RUNNING MY OWN SHOW

The Secrets Behind Party Plan Success

By Shirley McKinnon

CITY PRINTING
Perth, Western Australia

Publisher:
McKinnon Media Pty Ltd
PO Box 89, Bull Creek, Western Australia 6149

Copyright Shirley McKinnon 2008
First published 2008
www.shirleymckinnon.com
www.partyplantraining.com

IBSN 1434848388
EAN-13 9781434848383
Printed in Australia by City Printing, Perth.

Cover design by Ray Peters

I dedicate this book to every woman who takes the first step to become more of herself.
Who steps up to the bar to become the best she can be.
The world needs you. Your families need you.
And your teams need you as the great role models you are.

Included in this group of amazing women are my daughters Kelly and Angie. Each has faced her personal challenges with great courage, despite their fears and insecurities, to shine as great mothers and talented lights in the world.
You inspire me and fill me with great pride. I love you. You're awesome.

Acknowledgements

I would like to thank all the people who have contributed to this book by sharing with me what they felt were the biggest challenges they faced when they started in their party plan business. Some have identified their biggest challenge, others have pointed out what has been the most difficult to teach others, and others have simply participated in coaching either face-to-face or by phone.

I want to thank all the following people for their emails, conversations and their suggestions which have contributed towards this book. Some are old friends and we have been on a journey together for quite a few years while others are new.

Paula Couchman, Cindy Dinh, Shannon Jones, Maureen Mulligan, Jenni Smart, Liz Stockwell, Maree Swan, Effie Szalai, Marilyn Wallace-Harrison and Jenny Whyte.

And all those nameless friends who I have coached or who have approached me for advice and guidance on their party plan business. I have learned far more than you have gained from me by watching your courage, your determination, your self-discovery and the joy and excitement of your dreams coming true.

I'd also like to thank all those companies who allowed me to train their consultants and their Leaders either through workshops, conferences, boot camps or to be coaching as individuals; Nutrimetics, The Body Shop At Home, Enjo, Avon, Envy and The Learning Ladder. With special mention to Maureen Mulligan, previously of Mary Kay, Nutrimetics and now General Manager of The Learning Ladder. And to Mark Kindness, National Manager, The Body Shop At Home for inviting an outside trainer into your wonderful organisation.

Last but not least, my family who put up with the vacant mind while I'm writing, and the continuous discussions on what works and the endless details which make up the publication of a book. My darling husband Russell, my precious daughters and best friends, Kelly and Angie. Above all, my inspiration for what potential is all about, my granddaughters Amaria and Elizabeth, while Bo and Bailey are too young to appreciate their contribution yet.

Index

1

The Journey Begins

"You know, Sarah, I'm tired." Jenny poured Sarah a coffee and curled up in her favourite chair. "I'm tired of always not having enough money. Sick and tired of avoiding opening the mail, dreading the bills. I've become a coupon-cutting, bargain hunter and I'm fed up with it."

Sarah smiled. "I know what you mean. I'm a bit the same, although things have been a bit easier since Mum started looking after Jason and I started at the coffee shop. It's not my dream job, it's bloody hard work but it helps pay the bills."

Jenny closed her eyes. "You know, I used to have a life. BK. Before kids. I had a good job. And, I had money to spend on myself. Those were the days I used to buy accessories! My god, I bought a dress, a bag, earrings and shoes. All at once!"

"What do other people do to get ahead?" wondered Sarah. "Maybe we could start a little business together and make a million."

"Yeah, right! What could we do? And you need money to get started." Jenny was starting to feel depressed. She sat up and changed the subject. "At least we'll have some fun at Sandra's party tonight. I've told her I can't afford to buy anything, but I sure as hell can drink her wine!" She chuckled. It was dangerous to spend too much time wallowing in her problems. She felt down and couldn't see a way out. She was just so tired of going to the supermarket with a ridiculously tight budget, of never being able to buy what she wanted. Tired of making do. Tired of telling the girls they couldn't have things. She and Mark had talked about her getting a job, but until the girls started school, she couldn't see how it would work.

At Sandra's party, the lounge was covered in clusters of shoes and gorgeous bags. They were so different from the shoes she looked at in the shops. Sandra had said that they were Italian-designed but Jenny and Sarah weren't prepared for the range of unusual colours, the shoe bling. The bags were large and stylish, or small and elegant. Every look you wanted to create was here, waiting to be bought. Jenny decided she was going to pretend she could buy what she wanted, so was going to try everything on. She did that when she was shopping, she would window shop and pretend she could buy anything she wanted. As she tried on the shoes and admired herself in the mirror with a range of the leather bags, Jenny swung round and noticed a sign on the table, which stopped her in her tracks. "Want to earn some extra money? Talk to me."

She nudged Sarah and indicated the sign. "Hey, maybe we could sell shoes and bags."

"Wishful thinking, kid. We know nothing about them, let alone how to sell the stuff."

But as she listened to Sandra's spiel, it didn't seem to be that difficult. And Jenny watched the women's faces light up as they admired the shoes they tried on, finding the right size, deciding what colour to get. Jenny realised as Sandra took the orders that she was going to have sales of well over $1,000! She wondered how much of that would Sandra be earning? And she knew that Sandra had more parties booked for this week.

Sandra's voice brought her back to the present. "So remember, there are three ways you can get these gorgeous shoes and bags. You can buy them tonight. You can get some of them for free by having your own party. Or you can become a Rep."

Sandra came over to her and asked her if she wanted to place an order. "Actually, Sandra, the truth is I'm so broke. But what's this about getting free shoes if I have a party?" She looked enviously at the pair she had on. She hadn't had the heart to take them off yet, but she knew she had to give them back. Before she knew what had happened, she had booked a party. "And Sandra, I wouldn't mind hearing a bit about… you know, do you actually make much money doing this?" she blurted out.

Two days later, Sarah was barely in the door before Jenny started. Sarah had never seen Jenny so excited. "Do you know that Sandra will earn $1,300 this month from selling her shoes and bags? She is getting paid for having parties and having unlimited access to ranges of new shoes and handbags!"

"There's got to be a catch though. I mean, how much time does she spend on it?"

Jenny walked past her favourite chair and put her coffee on the table. Sarah followed her, a bit uneasy about where this was headed.

"She works the hours she wants while the kids are at school. When she has parties in the weekend, Jim minds the kids. And she earned $1,300 this month," she repeated. "What I could do with $1,300." She looked directly at Sarah. "Selling gorgeous shoes would be a damn sight better than working in that sweat shop you call a coffee shop!" Jenny leaned forward, an earnest look on her face. "Sarah, why don't we do this together?"

"What!" Sarah felt uneasy. She didn't share Jenny's excitement at all. It seemed too easy. There had to be a catch. "But we don't know anything about selling shoes or bags. Or what to do," she said with a catch of panic in her voice. She felt like she was being driven into a corner.

"Look, I'm having a party next week. Let's watch how it goes and we can pick Sandra's brain on how she got started. We can find out how much she has been earning since she started. I know they have a training programme, and you get weekly telephone coaching to get you started. And do you know what else?"

"What else could there be?" Sarah laughed. It was all a bit too much.

"She is working her way to their international conference. In Hawaii! And if she reaches her sales targets, she gets to take her husband too. For free! It's what she calls her five-star lifestyle."

"Now you're talking." Sarah sat forward. "Are you seriously telling me that she is getting a free trip to Hawaii?"

Sarah smiled. "And she earns $1,300 a month. With that amount coming in each month, I could clear those bills in no time."

They looked at each other grinning. "I want to run my own show," said Sarah. "I want to work my own hours, wear fabulous shoes, have fun at parties, become really good at it and build my own team. And I want to go to Hawaii. For starters." She looked up at the ceiling. "Hear that, Universe?"

Sarah's party was a great success. She was feeling more energetic than she could remember feeling since she had the kids. She had invited more than enough people as Sandra said that a few always dropped out, so she invited 15 and 10 turned up. Perfect. Sandra said that 10 was about the perfect number. She had wine, nibbles and watched closely as Sandra set up the bags on her dining room table. She arranged the large bags in clusters around the room. The smaller bags she tucked around the shoes. She had been slowly picking Sandra's brain every time she phoned to organise the party. Hostess coaching was what they called it. Jenny was more and more convinced that this was right for her and Sarah, and was a fun way out of their financial problems. She was really excited. And even more so when she saw the total of what had been sold at her party. She carefully went through the catalogue to choose what she could get for free, that she could use for selling. And she gave Sandra a firm commitment that she was going to join.

However, Mark had different ideas when she told him about paying the fee to join. To Jenny, it seemed worth it. You paid $500 on your credit card the first month, and $500 a month for the next two months. But you were earning money by then, so you would be covered. And she had a $500 gap on her card, just.

"Are you crazy? You've been sucked in big time! What scheme is this, anyway? Here we are, we can't even pay our bills and you're throwing away

$500 on shoes! You're unbelievable." He turned back to the TV in disgust, shaking his head.

"But Mark, I'll be earning money." Jenny was devastated.

"Yeah, right, I'll believe that when I see it." He turned the volume of the TV up higher. "I don't want to talk about it. I've heard about these schemes. Only the people who start them make any money."

"But it's not…"

The volume went up louder. Jenny phoned Sarah. "He won't even discuss it. And I'm just trying to help us get ahead."

"Are you sure you really want to do this?" asked Sarah.

"I'm sure. I really believe that this is the way out. Aren't you?" Jenny couldn't believe that Sarah might be backing out.

"I'm not quite sure yet. It looks good." But she didn't sound like she was that confident.

"Well, watch this space. Because we can make this work. Together, let's prove Mark wrong. We'll make him eat his words. Just watch."

The following week saw Sarah picking up Jenny to attend their first training session. Both were feeling apprehensive and were dreading the Rah! Rah! Rah! type training. Sarah was adamant. "If they do all the positive stuff, I'm out of there and out of the business. That kind of stuff just makes me want to puke!"

"Yes, well, I'm not that into that sort of stuff either. But let's see what happens before we make any decisions."

They were met at the door and a glance around the room revealed groups of women talking excitedly. Immediately they were allocated to Maria, whose job it was to show them round and make them comfortable. "Now, I know you'll be wondering what will be happening tonight, so I've got an agenda here for you to look at while I get you both a cup of coffee."

They sat down where Maria had indicated and both poured over the agenda. Recognition for those who had achieved over the past month, a talk from a top sales lady and a module on product knowledge. "This looks all good," Jenny was pleased. "These are all the things I want to know about. I'm happy with this."

"As long as they don't go over the top for the Recognition Session," Sarah added. When Maria returned with three coffees on a tray, she sat down next to them and explained a bit more about how the evening would go. Then she asked them if they had any questions for her. "How long have you been in J'Adore?" asked Jenny.

Maria didn't even have to think. She smiled, "Six months almost exactly. And I have just recruited my eighth person."

"Gosh, that's good going." Sarah was a bit taken back. "So what are you average party sales?"

4

"You two ask all the right questions," replied Maria. "Most people just want to know if you still love doing it. But the stats are the thing you really want to focus on." She reached under the chairs and handed them a white plastic folder each. "This is your training folder. There are sheets of paper in there for you to take notes on. And keep any handouts you get in there too. That way you know where all your tips and ideas are when you need them. There are some goal-setting sheets in there also which we will be doing tonight. Now, what was your question again?"

"What are your average party sales," asked Sarah again. "That's if you don't mind us asking."

"I'm pretty much sitting at $1,800 a party at the moment. And," she leaned forward towards Sarah, "don't apologise for asking questions. The more questions you ask, the more you learn. We're all pretty open about how we're doing here because we get so much encouragement from each other. So we all celebrate each other's wins as well. You'll love it. Just wait and see." She leaned forward again and lowered her voice. "In fact, tonight is really special. We are celebrating one lady's success, which is special to us all. Kelly had just got started and was going really well when she had a car accident. We all stepped in and did her parties for her until she got back on her feet. We all made sure we got bookings for her to keep her business going for her. She took a while to get back into it, but she has just recruited her first team member, despite still being in a bit of pain with her back. We are all so proud of her."

"You mean you all did her parties for her, and she got the sales? You did it for nothing?" Jenny couldn't believe that there was a group who could be this supportive.

"Of course. But it's not for nothing. She would have done the same for us. And it meant she had money coming in while she was recuperating. Try getting that to happen out there in the "real" business world. I don't think so!" Maria looked so pleased with herself. Jenny simply looked at Sarah, but the look said everything.

The recognition when it happened caught Jenny quite unawares. When Bella made her way on to the stage, the clapping from the audience of smiling women rose to a crescendo and as one, the whole group rose to their feet, clapping until their hands were sore. Jenny listened with tears in her eyes, as Bella described how she thought her career with J'Adore was over before it had really begun. She thanked all those who had run her parties for her from the bottom of her heart. The clapping started again when Bella introduced her new team member who was also sitting in the audience. Everyone who had done well that month was recognised. Those who had done exceptional sales, and those who had done their first party were all recognised and encouraged. Some won awards and seemed stunned by their success. So many said that if they could do it, then anyone could do it.

The presentation by the lady who had blitzed her sales targets for the previous month, had both Sarah and Jenny taking copious notes in the manual. And the product knowledge talked about the designers who were responsible for identifying and interpreting the latest Italian trends. By the end of the product knowledge module, Jenny felt much more confident about discussing the unusual styling of the shoes and bags, and where the ideas came from. She knew that this would become an addition to her presentation at the start of the party. That's why she loved J'Adore, because the shoes and bags were so unlike anything you could get in the shops. They were reasonably priced but they looked so stylish.

On the way home, they compared notes. "What was the best tip of the night for you?" asked Sarah as she drove out of the car park.

Sarah had to stop and think. "Gosh, I got so much out of tonight. I loved learning more about the bags and shoes and the story behind their design. But I think the thing which will add to my sales is the idea of laminating the list of all the benefits of joining the business for them to write on."

Sarah frowned. "I must have missed that. Tell me what that was."

"Well, you make up a form which lists all the benefits about joining the business. With a coloured pic of your favourite bags on there, of course. Then you get the form laminated, and you can use it instead of the clipboard, for them to lean on to fill out their wish list and their order. Some time during the party, they're bound to get the chance to read it."

"Are you really going to use the wish list?" Sarah seemed surprised. "I couldn't see the point to it myself. Why build them up for what they can't afford?"

"But, both Sandra and Maria have told us that that's how you get parties. If they can't afford what they want, suggest they have their own party so they get the hostess offer. I'm definitely going to try it."

They chatted all the way home, excited after mixing with so many women who seemed to be doing so well. It seemed to bode well for both their businesses.

"Don't forget to book next month's training session in your diary," Jenny reminded Sarah.

"I'll do it as soon as I get in," Sarah promised.

"I knew you hadn't done it," Jenny grinned. "Great night eh. I'm not going to have any trouble going along to nights like that. And if we can learn one thing at each session, it's really well worth it."

Sarah agreed and they parted both feeling so confident about their future, building a successful party plan business.

2
Coaching The Start Of The Journey

Congratulations! You have just embarked on an amazing learning journey. I know you think you have embarked on a new business or hobby. Either you want to build a new business or simply earn a bit more money, but you are going to learn lots about...you! Business is a great teacher. Right now you are feeling excited and enthusiastic. Probably a bit nervous and wondering if you've bitten off a bit more than you can chew. You've taken a very courageous step towards making your dreams and your ideal life come true. Well done and good for you. You have moved into an elite group of people which takes responsibility for creating dreams and making them come true. What happens over the next 12 months will reveal more about yourself than any self-development workshop you could possibly do.

You will have days where you are optimistic and you move forward, in action. You will have other days where you have good intentions but no action. You will have to face what you don't like and have to do some things you don't want to do. And whether you respond or react will dictate your level of success. Respond by learning new skills and being prepared to stretch your comfort zone, and your business will grow. React by blaming anything outside of yourself for your results, and like so many others before you, you will probably use those excuses to walk away.

So, let's face these challenges together. I'll be your mentor, your coach, your teacher, your guide and your cheerleader. The great thing is that in this industry, you are encouraged to make mistakes. Unlike going to school or being in mainstream business, where you are taught to avoid making mistakes, you will not be successful in the direct selling unless you are prepared to make lots of mistakes. Because mistakes show that you are <u>doing</u> something. And in this industry, action allied with planning, is everything.

Action without planning is chaos. Planning and good intentions without action is a very slow way to success. But great for sitting around with your friends chatting about what you are going to do, and then finding that because of the time spent having the coffee, you don't have time to do what you intended to do. But at least you "felt" like you were being busy.

Too many people judge how they are doing by how they feel.

Too many people judge how they are doing by how they feel. When they talk about their plans and their intentions, they feel like they are putting planning into action. Complaining is like a stress pill, it makes you feel better but nothing changes. If you have doubts, do something. Just act. If you feel like you are getting nowhere, do something. Just act. If you feel de-motivated, do something. Just act. If you can follow the following advice — you can't go wrong! Your success is assured. I would highly recommend that you repeat this every day for the first two weeks. And then every time your motivation wanes or you face a challenge or disappointment.
- I act in spite of fear.
- I act in spite of doubt.
- I act in spite of worry.
- I act in spite of inconvenience.
- I act in spite of discomfort.
- I act when I'm not in the mood.

Most people who turn their backs on their party plan business fail because they failed to act. If you focus on massive action while you are enthusiastic, and then focus on the results to fine tune that action — you can't go wrong. It might not feel like you are doing well, but as I said before, in this industry, you learn as you go along. And there are enough people out there, so that if you stuff up and don't do that good at a party, there's plenty more where they came from.

One last word on intention and action from the great American basketball coach, John Woodden. "Intentness doesn't involve wanting something. It involves doing something. Be persistent. Be determined. Be tenacious. Be completely determined to achieve your goal. That's intention."

"Intentness doesn't involve wanting something. It involves doing something.
Be persistent. Be determined. Be tenacious.
Be completely determined to achieve your goal. That's intention."

The Direct Selling Industry

When you start your own party plan business, one of the first challenges you will face is your friends' and possibly your partner's reactions. It's wise to prepare yourself for a bit of an emotional roller coaster. You'll start full of confidence and full of dreams. You'll be enthusiastic and passionate about your products. You'll be motivated to achieve your goals. You'll feel like you have joined a warm and supportive community, and that's exactly what you will have done if you've joined one of the good companies. So, it often comes as a shock to discover that either your partner and/or your friends and family, are cynical about your move. And not just cynical, some people will be openly scornful and critical about you joining the party plan industry. So, let's have a look at what is going on here.

Firstly, so many people are utterly unaware of what a huge, virtual industry the party plan and direct-selling industry is. Their opinion is coloured by horror stories of pyramid selling and people who dropped out, left with garages filled with unsold product. And the reality is, that this couldn't be further from the truth. BRW Magazine claims that an estimated 630,000 people are involved at some level in direct selling in Australia, making the industry a substantial provider of incomes.

And this is not a new industry. I can remember as a child, my mother buying Rawleigh's products, which a man sold door to door carrying his products in a large wicker basket. Its pink tonic for upset tummies was the best on the market. And, if my memory serves me well, they also carried a range of household cleaning and cooking products. Rawleigh's claim was that it had been in business since the 18th Century!

Avon started in America in 1886. *Today, it is a $7.7 billion company and has almost five million representatives in more than 100 countries. Each year, women earn close to $3 billion selling Avon. With 17 million brochures going out every two weeks, Avon is the second largest publisher in the United States after TV Guide.

Mary Kay turned a $5,000 investment into a billion-dollar make-up corporation, which has helped thousands of women launch successful careers. Her Go-Give culture with its mission To Enrich Women's Lives is typical of the focus most party plan companies place on training and empowering women to take control of their lives and their finances without sacrificing quality family time.

Tupperware has been in business for more than 50 years and claims to be one of the world's leading direct-selling companies with nearly one million independent salespeople in more than 100 countries.

Nutrimetics has been in business for more than 37 years and aims to give people the opportunity to position their work around their lives and not their lives around their work. A household name, which has grown to become one of Australia's and New Zealand's leading skin-care companies, it has

*Andrea Jung, Chairman and Chief Executive Officer, Avon Products, Inc. in *Avon, Building the World's Premier Company for Women* by Laura Klepacki

more than 200,000 consultants worldwide.

And when a company with such a formidable reputation for business ethics and integrity such as The Body Shop created a party plan company, The Body Shop at Home, you know that party plan has become an integral part of women's lives. The rest of the business world just hasn't realised it yet. And yet, some studies have predicted that one third of all goods and services will be moved via direct sales and network marketing in western nations this century, and this could be as high as 50 percent in developing nations by 2110.

In fact, right now, you can buy just about any product from party plan and direct-selling companies, including educational children's books, make-up, health-care products such as vitamins and other wellness-related products; jewellery; storage containers including microwave cookware; pots and pans; lingerie and adult toys to name just a few.

Services such as Customer Kitchen Planning and telephone services are offered through party plan, while some companies also include group discounts for insurance and travel by creating partnerships with mainstream businesses. While direct selling in Australia is a $1 billion a year industry, it is a "virtual" industry which the majority of people are quite unaware of.

Comfort Zones

Everyone has dreams they would like to achieve. We all dream of a better life. However, some people stay doing exactly that, dream about it, while others get their act together and work towards achieving their dreams and goals. So when you start learning something new, in an industry that some people know little about, they only see the risk, the unknown, the threat of change of doing something different. And they focus on the possibility of failure. And by doing nothing, they think they are avoiding failure. In fact, they are demonstrating it.

However, when you create and move towards new goals, you are reflecting to them what is possible. What happens when you have the courage and passion to commit yourself to the unknown and learn new skills, you discover new talents. You will create discomfort in their lives and you may find friends and family will react quite strongly to what you are doing. It is easier to criticise you than it is to turn and face their frustrated desires. Just remember, this is their stuff, not your reality.

Just remember, this is their stuff, not your reality.

Never underestimate how strong some people's comfort zones

are. It can keep them immobilised while they struggle financially, suffer emotionally and experience a range of unhappy experiences. But they will still be full of bad advice for anyone who starts something new. Here's your benchmark of whether you listen to their advice or politely ignore it. Look at them and ask yourself: "Are they a great role model for my life?"

"Are they a great role model for my life?"

If the answer is no, you do not want to copy what they do, what they think or absorb their opinions. Move on. Leave them to their opinions and their problems.

The Reality Of Self-Responsibility

While you are flush with optimism and enthusiasm, really go for it. Book as many parties as you can, talk to as many people as possible and get the most mileage from that first burst of energy. However, I would recommend that when you get started, don't ask your friends "to have a party". Ask them "to support you in your new business by having a party". It's much harder to say no to supporting you than it is to say no to having a party. But at the same time, be prepared for some close friends who you are confident will hold a party for you, to not just say no, but to be a bit derisive about it. The first time it happens, it is a bit of a shock.

When you first start, your energy will drive you forward effortlessly so it's a good idea to take advantage of it and book as many parties as you can while you're still high on motivation. Because sooner or later you are going to be faced with the reality that all the results you get, are a direct result of the efforts you put in. It might have seemed like the sales just happened at those first parties you saw, but everything that consultant was doing either added to, or undermined her sales. It looks effortless, but everything she said and everything she had prepared before the party, actually dictated what her sales were going to be.

It's the same with booking parties. If you get "too busy" to follow up leads, you won't book more parties. If you get "too busy" you won't be prepared and maximise your sales. Your business and your sales, will not just happen. You determine the degree of the momentum of your business. Your activities determine your results. You ease off, your sales and party bookings will slow down. You get distracted and your sales and your party bookings will slow down. It's got nothing to do with the company, the products, the economy or your neighbourhood, your friends or their friends. It has everything to do with you!

Prepare yourself for the fact that life will get in the road as you pursue your dreams. It's not the case of IF something turns up to distract you, but

WHEN it does. If you are focused and repeating the Act Affirmation at the start of this chapter, you will find a way to continue despite life throwing all sorts of distractions and hurdles at you.

Attending Training

Your upline and all the people who run the training, were where you are at now at the beginning of their party plan career. While they might look confident and successful to you, that's not the way it always was for them. Like you, they struggled and felt out of their depth. They had little confidence and didn't feel like they knew what they were doing. But one of the things you can guarantee was that they all attended as many of the monthly training sessions as possible. It is really important for you to try to do this also.

Firstly, you mix with people who are doing well. You can ask them questions, get ideas and tips. Unlike other areas of business, they will happily share with you the main techniques or strategies that they found worked for them. Every person seems to discover one thing that made a difference to their sales, their bookings or their recruiting. You get to rub shoulders with great role models, although few see themselves as this. When they look back at when they started, they see the struggle, the lack of confidence and all the mistakes they made at the start of their business.

Secondly, you get recognition for your progress. Now, in Australia and New Zealand, this can be an uncomfortable thought and they prefer to remain as quiet achievers. But can't you see, you are inspiring those who haven't really got their businesses started yet? If you've only recently started and you've had good sales and bookings, think how motivating and encouraging that is for other new people. You see, while you are independent and running your own business, the beauty of party plan is that you have also now become part of a team. You gain energy and motivation from seeing others' success, and they gain energy and motivation from your success.

Thirdly, you will learn product knowledge and techniques, which will increase your confidence. Every training session should add to your knowledge. You will find that you are more confident in talking about the products and I often find that you may learn as much by chatting to others at the training session, as you do from the actual training module.

You will also feel fully supported. Others around you will encourage you and tell you their stories. Explaining the mistakes they have made, the new techniques they've tried. But notice how they simply tell you about it, even laugh about it. No wallowing from them. They have moved on.

Last but not least, you will come away from the training feeling energised with a new determination and focus. There's nothing like a training session to get your focus back on achieving your goals. If you were to get nothing else each month than renewed focus, a fresh burst of energy and determination, it would be worth it. But you get so much more. You get so much knowledge, tips and techniques. You are bound to increase sales even if you only apply a few tips of what you learn. This is one of the great pluses of the party plan industry. Everyone is so generous in sharing what has worked for them. Everyone is so excited at your successes, no matter how small and wish to share them with you. I'm sorry, but if you have a part-time job, just don't expect to get this same support. It is almost unique to a few sales teams, and most all of the party plan industry.

Action

Commit yourself to attending every training session. Make it a high priority. Go and book those sessions right now into your diary. Don't wait and see how you are feeling on the day, how busy that day is. Book it into your diary and if it's in your diary, it happens!

NOTES

NOTES

NOTES

3

Take Massive Action

After Sandra had left, carrying their signed joining forms, Jenny and Sarah looked at each other and grinned. "I can't believe we've done it," said Sarah.

"I know, it's great!" Jenny opened the drawer and pulled out a large diary. "I bought this yesterday. Sandra said to try and attend every training session we can, and that's exactly what I'm going to do." She started marking in the training sessions each month.

"Gosh, you're organised. I'll have to get one, too."

"Can't wait to book in my first parties. Mum has agreed to have one. You can hold one for me, and I'll have one for you. That's two for me. Sandra says to get four booked in, so I'm going to book in six. Every target they give me, I'm going to do more. I'm really determined to do this."

Sarah stood up. "Well, I'm off. I said I'd meet Marilyn for coffee."

Jenny looked at her in astonishment. "But don't you want to get home and start booking parties?"

"There's plenty of time for that. I can do that later. Anyway, maybe Marilyn will have one if I ask her."

As soon as Sarah had left, Jenny wrote out a list of all the people she knew she could ask to have a party. If any said that they couldn't this month, she was going to put them at the start of next month. Anyway, why wouldn't they when the parties were so much fun. In this state of mind, she started phoning.

That night, she phoned Sarah. She was so excited. "How did you go with Marilyn today?"

"Yeah, good. We had coffee and chatted for a while. Why?"

"Did you ask her to have a party for you?"

"Yes, I did. I couldn't believe it, she said no! I felt terrible."

"That's strange. I would've thought that Marilyn would have been a starter. Did she say why?"

"Yes, she's got her in-laws visiting. So she's tied up with cooking dinners and showing them around."

"Well, that's okay then. That doesn't mean no, it just means no for now. Ask her again after they've left, she'll probably have one then." Jenny's enthusiasm wasn't diminished at all. But Sarah wasn't feeling good about asking people to have these parties.

"I don't know Jenny. I died when she said no. I don't think I could ask her again."

"Don't be silly," Jenny scolded her. "I've been on the phone all afternoon. While you've been having coffee." She couldn't resist having a dig. "And I've got three more parties booked. On top of Mum's one and your one! I'm on my way."

Somehow, Jenny's success only made Sarah feel worse. But she knuckled under and the next morning got on the phone and started making phone calls. She felt really uncomfortable. It seemed like she was "using" her friendship to get people to have parties. But when she told them about the Italian shoes, the Vogue-style bags, how gorgeous they were and how much fun they had at the parties, two of her friends booked. She was over the moon. She found that the more people she asked, the less bad she felt about it. And with Jenny checking her progress, she just kept going until she had her four parties booked. Sarah was relieved.

The day of Jenny's first party arrived and she was nervous and excited at the same time. She kept thinking she didn't really know what she was doing, but Sandra was going to do the first party for her, so she really just had to listen and learn. She had spent the last couple of days going over the party script and trying to learn it. She'd dipped into the manual but there seemed so much there and it had been a busy week for the kids. They had sports day coming up and Sinead had her dancing competitions coming up. That meant costumes and lots of panic and time consumed getting it right. Sinead was so like her father. Everything had to be just right. And the sheer terror of getting the wrong lipstick, the wrong colour of dress, the wrong hairstyle — it was a nightmare.

She had moved some of the furniture around so Sandra could better layout the bigger bags, which were so popular at the moment and made sure that everyone could see the table. She had bought some stands on which she could present the shoes. Sandra said that the more people could try the shoes on, the more they would buy. And Jenny wanted them to try on lots!

She had some nibbles and wine ready. As she was putting on her make-up and getting ready, it crossed her mind to wonder what the successful entrepreneur would be wearing. She didn't have to worry about Mark as this was his poker night. His night with the boys. But she was hoping that when he came home, she would be able to tell him that she'd had a great sales night. She really had to turn him around.

She watched closely as Sandra set up and asked questions on why she displayed some shoes one way and others quite differently. Sarah arrived early but went straight into hostess mode and was offering and pouring wine as others arrived. There was a catalogue and a wish list for every person. Jenny wasn't sure what the wish list was for. But she made sure that every person had a pen. How can you fill out your wish list if you didn't have a pen?

People started straggling in about 15 minutes early. Some had got their kids into bed and just left. It seemed that some women had so little time away from their kids, that they were starved for adult company. But Jenny noticed, that so many of them then spent their whole evening talking about their kids. When do women get time for themselves without their families taking priority, she wondered. In fact, Jenny wanted to make this party really special for her guests. She wanted them to relax, have a good time and spoil themselves for a few hours. She made a mental note to talk to Sandra to see how she could make this a really fun, nurturing party.

Jenny was disappointed that of the 10 who were invited and had confirmed their attendance, only seven turned up. However, once everyone was there, Sandra introduced herself and the chatting slowed to a murmur, then ceased. She explained who she was and a bit about the history of the company. She talked about why she joined J'Adore, and Jenny noticed how people turned and smiled at each other in sympathy as Sandra explained some of the problems she had been struggling with prior to joining the company. Amazed, Jenny realised that in this short introduction, Sandra had connected with the women. They could totally relate to what she was saying. And while she didn't quite know why, she knew that this was a really important thing to do.

When she stopped and thought about it, standing in front of a group of strangers was probably one of the most daunting things for new people. That would be the one thing they thought they couldn't do. And everyone looking at how professional Sandra was, would be surprised to know that she had probably been as nervous as Jenny was now when she first started. So when Sandra identified herself as one of them, with kids and money problems just the same as them, they not only warmed to her, they started to realise that she was simply one of them. Some would therefore be thinking, gosh, if she can do this, maybe I could to. She was beginning to understand how much the introduction was an important part of the whole sales process. Revealing your vulnerability, introducing your self and your family, explaining why you joined party plan, presented you as just another mother who was trying to solve problems. It took you from the realms of being "so together" and professional into their world, of kids, money problems and nothing to wear,

Jenny realised.

Next, Sandra started talking about the shoes and the bags. Jenny noticed that she was asking a few questions of the ladies and involving them in conversations about their wardrobe, the look they would like to have. And, as she started to explain about the shoes and describe them, she started passing shoes around for them to touch and try on. Jenny noticed how some of the women almost stroked the shoes, touching them with reverence. Somehow, the Italian design made them special. More desirable than the shoes most of them would normally buy. And the great thing was that while they were so much more stylish, they actually didn't cost much more. Jenny had put shoes on layby, which were much more expensive than these.

The noise level had now gone up considerably. In fact, you wouldn't have been able to hear Sandra if she was still talking. But she wasn't. She was going around and talking individually to each of the people. And to Jenny's excitement, she was taking orders. Then people started asking Jenny some questions. Some she could answer, others she had to go and ask Sandra. But it made her feel like she was really in the business. She loved it. So she also continued to go around the room and talk to each of the ladies. She encouraged them to try on what they wished they could buy. To every person who said they couldn't afford what they wanted, or said perhaps they could get some once they had paid some bills, she suggested they have their own party so they could get what they wanted at half-price. Sarah continued to refill drinks and look after everyone.

The evening flew by and after the guests had all left, Sandra and Jenny added up the sales — $735. And she had two more party bookings.

"While you want to concentrate on getting good sales, you must make a real effort to get bookings," explained Sandra. "This is the only way you can grow your business, through party bookings. Try to make a goal of getting a minimum of two party bookings at each party. Put together incentives, offers to entice them to have a party if they are considering having one of their own. Without parties in the pipeline, you have no business. It's as straight forward as that."

Although it was getting late, Jenny continued to pick Sandra's brain and find out why she did some things a certain way while Sarah cleared the dishes and stacked them in the sink. After Sandra had gone, they planned their next parties together. Sarah made a discreet exist when Mark returned home.

"Well, how did it go? Any sales?" Mark got himself a beer and sat down turning on the TV. Jenny picked up the controls and turned off the TV. "$735 actually, and we need to talk about this."

"$735? That's pretty good isn't it?" Mark sat up a bit straighter.

"Well, I guess it's not bad for a first party, but quite a few of the girls are doing $1,000 parties and the highest has been over $3,000."

Mark was now listening. "So how much money would you make from a $1,000 party?"

Jenny picked up the brochure on the incentive scheme and walked Mark through the possibilities of what she could earn if she took this business seriously. She showed him her plan of three to four parties a week. She showed him what goals she had set and outlined what she intended to do with the money she would be earning. Mark listened quietly. Then he turned to her. "Are you sure this is for real? I mean, the company's not going to pay out that much commission, surely!"

Jenny shared with him what some of the women were making. "But I have to become good at booking parties, and then I have to learn to recruit. Because once I have a team, I get a percentage of their sales as well. Look." Jenny walked him through the concept of the down line team.

"And you like doing this?" Mark asked.

"Are you kidding me? Holding parties, wearing shoes to die for, bags that turn others green with envy, and making money. It doesn't get better than that as far as jobs go. I love it. I can't wait to get my next party happening to see what my sales will be."

Mark sat back. "Is there anything I can do to help?"

Jenny looked at him and could feel the prickle of tears in her eyes. "Thank you. I know you didn't like the idea to begin with, but knowing that you'll support me in this means a lot to me. After all, this is a business and I want to treat it like one."

"Well," Mark looked thoughtful, "if you're really serious about this business, and if you can earn that kind of money, I'll support you, sure as hell. Why don't we turn the spare room into an office? We can move the spare bed into Sinead's room and we could get a cheap desk and shelves. What do you think?"

Jenny leaned forward and wrapped her arms around him. "Thank you. I know I can do this. And wouldn't it be great to get to conference together, paid for by the company! And one last thing, Sandra says that the women who are the most successful at party plan, are the ones who have their husbands and families behind them. So, you've just helped me become more likely to be successful just by supporting me. Now all I have to do is to get the kids to be a bit less demanding. As if!"

"Tell you what," Mark grinned. "Let's have a family meeting tomorrow. Put it to the kids and involve them in supporting you as well."

Jenny was glowing. How good was this. If she could earn a great living from this business and she had her family supporting her, she had it made.

However, her sense of good fortune quickly changed.

It all started with Sinead reminding her of her dance concert. On the same night as her training night. Jenny couldn't believe it. She had started with such good intentions and already her family was taking priority over her business. She couldn't see how she could miss either of them. She tried sounding out Sinead on how important if was for her to turn up. "Mum! I know what you're trying to do. You're trying to get out of coming and watching me. You promised!" And that seemed to be the end to that.

She phoned Sarah the next day. "Any suggestions? I've got Sinead's dance concert the same night as training. What am I going to do?"

"Go to Sinead's concert. Surely there's no question. Family comes first. Every time." Sarah's unhesitating sense of priorities made Jenny feel guilty. But she had so much to learn and she didn't want to miss training. It had become too important to her.

"It's not fair!" she said through gritted teeth over the ironing the next night. "I spend so much time doing things for my family that I can't get to what I want to do." Like every other mother in creation, she thought. Right, how can I be at both, she asked herself. I need to be at both. And then she had an idea. She raced out into the kitchen and pulled the Concert Programme from under its magnet on the door of the fridge. She scanned the programme, and, fingers crossed, called Sinead.

"What?"

"Sinead, don't speak to me in that tone. I'm not going to miss you dancing. Nothing in the world is more important than that." Jenny was quite firm on this.

Sinead straightened up and walked into the kitchen. "Good, 'cos you promised."

"And I will be there. But I need to ask you a favour. You're the third act on the programme. Would you be really upset if I miss the rest of the concert? You know that it's my training night and it's really important to me, too." Jenny held her breath.

"Yeah, that's hell sick. Whatever."

Jenny blinked. "What? What did you just say?"

Sinead tried not to grin. "Mum, keep up with the lingo. That means yes, all right?"

Jenny dived forward and gave her stunned daughter a big hug and a smacking kiss on the cheek.

"Ooh, Mum!!" Sinead protested but if truth be told, she had it both ways. She had Mum watching her dance, and she was allowing her to race away to her training. That should come in handy, having Mum owing her one.

At the concert, she was so proud of Sinead. She couldn't believe that the powerful dancer on stage had once been her little girl. She'd been pretty much in tears through the whole performance. Mark wasn't dry-eyed either. He was sneakily wiping his eyes behind the video camera when Jenny leaned across, gave him a quick kiss and took off. They had sat on the end seats so she could leave without disrupting other parents. However, she copped some disapproving looks on the way out.

Training was halfway through when Jenny raced through the door. She scanned the room for Sarah hoping that she would have saved her a seat but couldn't see her in the sea of heads. So she just slipped into the back row and took out her folder to make notes.

It seemed to be nearing the end of one presentation.

"So, you don't have to know everything before you have your first party. So many people think they need to study up on the product and know everything before they will even consider having a party. There is no problem with telling people you have just started and don't know all the answers. In fact, I recommend that you do exactly that in your presentation, tell them you are new at this. It helps your sales because some of them want to help you get started." There was a ripple of laughter around the room. Several people nodded their heads in agreement.

"It's the same with recruiting. Don't wait until you have been doing parties for six months before you start recruiting. Recruit straight away, at every party. How do you know that at your next party, there might be a very talented Manager just waiting to get into the business. And push yours through the roof! I have made a mint off leads that consultants handed on because they did not see the value of recruiting until they were more experienced. Overcome your reluctance and start recruiting straight away. It's surely one way to give your business a real kick start."

The last presenter talked about controlling the party. "When we do a party, we are really friendly with everyone, and therefore think we are talking to friends. So we become very passive and listen to them, and allow them to control us and the party. Once you have completed the presentation, your job ...." She repeated this with emphasis, "Your job is to take the orders, and politely slip away. Always set a time limit for yourself and stick to it. Do not be the last person to leave, it's not your party. It's your job. If you allow yourself to stay and chat as if you were a guest, you'll always be late home and you'll be drained the next day."

"That's what I used to do." The lady next to Jenny whispered.

"It's what I've been doing, too," replied Jenny. "But, you know I never thought about it. I just assumed that you had to stay." Another thing to learn how to do, she thought. "But from now on, I'm going to control my time at the party myself," she promised herself.

The next day, she got on the phone to Sarah. "Sarah, were you at training last night? I didn't see you."

"Did you go? I thought you were going to see Sinead's concert. Don't tell me you didn't go. Jenny, you're getting a bit obsessive about this business idea." Sarah's tone was stern and disapproving.

"Of course, I didn't miss it. I watched her and then raced to training. Where were you?"

"Well, I didn't think you were going. I didn't like the idea of going in on my own. So I didn't go."

"Oh, Sarah. You missed so much good stuff. Do you want to come over and go over my notes so you can catch up?"

"No thanks. I have to prepare for my party. I will be doing the party rather than talking about techniques and stuff. I'll be fine."

"Oh, Sarah." Jenny felt so helpless.

4

Coaching For Massive Action

When you first join party plan, it is important to do two things. One is to use that first surge of enthusiasm to dive in and create massive action. This fresh energy and excitement will compensate for the lack of skill you have at this stage. People will be attracted to your energy and the passion you have for your product. They want to be around passionate people in a world where mediocre is the standard. So before you really know what you are doing, your enthusiasm will make the difference.

Use that first surge of enthusiasm to dive in and create massive action.

When you surf that first surge of energy, you won't get tired or as discouraged as quickly. So you'll surge forward and people will be inspired by your enthusiasm and many will agree to hold a party for you. If someone has a valid reason for not holding a party, make a note in your diary at the start of next month to approach them and ask again. You want to get to the point where at the start of every month, you have a list of contacts who are possibles for parties. This means that you don't start your month feeling a bit desperate for ideas or who to ask for parties.

Set goals, plan your time and decide what you have to stop doing.

The second thing you need to be doing is understand that you need to change your timetable. If you want to start a business, you will need to learn to run a business even though party plan does not seem like a business. When you want something new in your life, you have to be prepared to sacrifice some other activities. Like less TV, not flicking through new magazines, chatting aimlessly to friends on the phone, meeting for coffee with no other agenda than to catch up. Everything you do now will either move you towards your goal or away from it. You are either wasting time or spending time.

Everything you do now will either move you towards your goal or away from it.

You are either wasting time or spending time.

Wasting time means that the pastime may be pleasurable, but it has not contributed to either your growth or the growth of your business. Spending time means that you are investing the time in your future. It's the difference between flicking through a magazine that you will throw away when you have finished, and reading through the manual, which comes with your products. One is a fleeting pleasure while the other educates and informs you and contributes ultimately to the success of your business.

When you set your goals, which is where your motivation, your energy and your focus comes from, you should also identify what you are prepared to give up or stop doing so you can achieve your goals. You will either learn to become more organised and use your time more productively, or you will get into overwhelm quite quickly.

Booking Parties — The Wrong Way

When most people join party plan, they phone their friends and the call goes something like this.

"Hi Sonia, how are you going?"

"Yeah, good, How about you?"

"Fantastic! I've just joined XYZ company and started my own business and I'm so excited, the products are great. Have you heard of them?" (*Loaded question.*)

"Yes, I think Roselle was doing their parties for a while. But she dropped out. I don't think she really had enough time. How come you've got involved?"

"I saw how much you can earn and there are overseas trips. But the products are fabulous. Have you ever seen them?" (*Another loaded question.*)

"No, I heard that they're great, though."

"Well, now that I've joined, I thought that you might like to have a party." Followed quickly by, "You'd have a great time. You only need about 10 people max and nibbles and drink while you shop is all good."

Sonia, now feeling uneasy and cornered, says: "I'd really like to but it's a really bad time for me at the moment. I hope it all goes well for you but I've got all the kids' sport at the moment and Jack's Mum is coming to stay. It's just too much. Maybe next month."

Let's have a look at what is going on here. No wonder party plan, direct selling and MLM get such a bad name. Poor Sonia, she felt like every question was going to trap her into having a party. And ask yourself this one question, what's in it for her to have a party? She can help her friend make money and get an overseas holiday! What an incentive. And because there's nothing in it for her, she will simply focus on all the negatives. She will think about having to phone her friends and ask them to a party, which she isn't that enthusiastic about anyway. She's got to shop for nibbles and drinks, let alone what it's going to cost her. She's got to organise the night, do something with husband and kids. And why should she? At the end of the day, she is a busy housewife and mother, and her evenings are when she collapses with some time for herself. You're asking a lot of her when you ask her to have a party. She's got no reason to agree.

Booking Parties — The Right Way

Let's look at a different approach to this phone call.
"Hi Sonia, how are you going?"
"Yeah, good, How about you?"
"Fantastic! I've just joined XYZ company and they have the best products."
Describe the products as if she was using them. Paint a picture she can relate to.
"They have these great storage containers, which keep food fresh in the kitchen. When you've got leftovers, you can keep them fresh in the fridge and use them the next day. No messing around with strips of cling wrap. And they stack in your fridge so you can have much more in there without filling the fridge to overflowing. Plus you can easily see what is in them. Really smart for busy women like us with hungry kids and full fridges."
Or
"This jewellery is real silver and gold, but instead of diamonds, they contain high quality zirconias. It is Italian designed, which means it is utterly stylish but costs so much less than you'd expect."
Or
"They've started this great experience like a day spa at home where you can sit back and have an evening with friends relaxing and trying beautiful products that really rejuvenate your skin."
"Wow, it sounds really good."
Now add, what's in it for her if she were to have a party.
"And the hostess gifts are amazing! It's what I really like about having the parties — how the company looks after and appreciates the hostess."
"Why, what do they get?" *Buying signal, showing some interest.*
"Well, according to the sales of the party, it's quite possible that the hostess gets several hundred dollars of (be specific about exactly what

products they would get for being a hostess) for free. And for every $100 spent, she also gets a free gift on top of that. In fact, our new free gift is so good, that some people are buying the products just to get the free gift. How about we get together for a coffee and I'll show you the catalogue and the free gift? And you know what I'm going to ask. Will you support me and have a party?" (*Notice she's not asking her to have a party, but asking her to support her. It's harder to say no to support than it is to say no to a party.*)

"Of course I will. Go on then, bring the catalogue over and let me have a look at these gorgeous things."

"Thank you, I really appreciate this. And you know, when you end up wearing these gorgeous shoes, carrying the stunning bags which look like they are straight out of Vogue, you may want to think about this as a part-time job yourself!" (*Planting the seed for recruiting. Already!*)

Buying Signals — Taking Orders At Your Parties

One of the reasons you have to watch and listen carefully to your customers for, is to pick up the Buying Signals. You see, once we like something and want it, we send out signals for the person selling the products, which say: "I'm ready to purchase. Ask me to buy. Take my order". When that person doesn't respond to our signals, we think they're not interested in us or our business. And all this is going on while we are not consciously aware of it.

Once we like something and want it, we send out signals for the person selling the products, which say: "I'm ready to purchase. Ask me to buy. Take my order."

What is the range of buying signals? When they pick up the products and try them on for starters. When they pick up the brochures and start flicking through them, searching for something they'd like. Questions such as whether it comes in a certain colour, how long the delivery is, and any questions about payment such as do you take credit card, or can I pay you on delivery, are all buying signals. And do you know what you do when you hear a buying signal? You take their order!

You go over to them with your order forms, and ask them what colour did they want it in? What size were they after? And you take their order.

Why do we miss buying signals? Because when we first get into direct selling, we feel vulnerable. We feel like people are having parties as a favour to us. What we miss is what is happening to our customers because we are so focused on what is happening to us. We miss that they have a party because of what they are going to get out of it — hostess gifts and the products they love. But because we are feeling vulnerable, we let them ask about colour, size, delivery and payment, and answer their questions but don't take their order. We don't realised that we have just taken away our support in the buying process just at the time they were making a commitment. We pulled the mat out from under them. And I have even heard them actually ask, "Can I please place an order?" before the person doing the selling gets the picture.

More buying signals are questions about parties and/or the business side of things. Questions such as:

"How many people do you need to invite for a party?"

"What sort of food would you have at an afternoon party?"

"How much does it cost to join?"

"Is there a payment plan for joining? Or do you have to pay all at once?"

"What kind of training do you get?"

"How long would it take before you start earning money?"

These questions are being asked because the person is imagining joining the business. These are buying signals. Whenever you get any questions such as these, you answer the question and then make a time to have a coffee with them to answer any further questions they may have. And then you invite them to join the business.

Most people miss buying signals because they can't believe what they're hearing. Some people have a natural ability to read buying signals and respond naturally without even realising this is what they're doing. But when you first start, because you feel so vulnerable in the role of selling, you want to train yourself to watch your customers closely, listen carefully to what they say, and train yourself to identify the buying signals. And respond accordingly. The more you identify and respond to them, the more it will come naturally. Eventually, you won't even notice you are doing it and it becomes almost a natural dance between you and your customers, satisfying to both sides of the sale.

Involve Your Family

When you start you business, most women dive in and assume they have to do it on their own. They try to keep up their original schedule, keep up with all the family demands and do everything they need to for their business. Remember, you are already a busy person. Well, most of you are. If

you are going to start a new business, there are three things you need to do:
1) Identify what things you will now not have time for
2) Attempt to get the full support of your family
3) Set up your office

1) Identify what things you will now not have time to do.

This may be spending time shopping with friends, reading magazines, watching TV, doing things for people which you have done in the past but will resent doing now if it takes time from your business. You may have volunteered much of your time to schools, sporting clubs and charities. It's time to put your business first and recognise that to be successful, you will have to change your timetable. I'm not saying that you need give up everything, but it's a good idea to warn people that you have started up your own business and are now going to have less time for other activities. This puts them on notice that if they are looking for volunteers, you may not now be the first choice as you have been in the past. Sometimes we get into the habit of doing things with someone and don't know how to stop. You now have your perfect excuse for anything you don't want to do. "Sorry, there are some things I need to do in my business."

2) Attempt to get the full support of your family

Call a family meeting. If you have never done this before, then it's about time you started. Call everyone together and tell them what you want to do. But more importantly, tell them *why* you want to do it. The why is more important than the what. Always. Let them hear about your dreams and goals. And why you want to achieve them. Paint them a picture of what life will be like for the family when you are successful. What's In It For Me — WIIFM (you'll see this phrase a lot in this book. People are not usually interested in what you want in life, but they are intensely interested in getting something for themselves.) Describe what they will get if you are successful. It might be a new skateboard, more money to spend on things they want (be specific), or it could be a family holiday, a trip to Disneyland. Whatever it is, you want to paint a clear picture of what life will be like for the family when you are successful. Ask them what they think, what they would like to see the family do together. Get their contribution.

However, in order to do this, some things will have to change. Tell them about the new demands on your time and what activities you aren't now going to have time for. Get their suggestions on how the family can support you in achieving your goals. Get them to make suggestions on what they can do to support you. You may be surprised. Write this all down in a notebook, who has agreed to do what. Bring this book out every time you have a family meeting. Reread what was written last time and see how they are going.

It is most important to let them come up with ideas and contribute.

The fact of the matter is that the family will be much more supportive of you if they understand what your vision and goals are. If they feel included, they will want to help. You can even bring the family closer through this process.

But if you haven't included them in your plans, all they will see is what they are losing. Your attention and all the things you do for them now. And they won't understand why they should change to fit in with your plans.

3) Set up your office

If you are serious about making this a business, ideally you need a place to work. Converting a spare bedroom into an office is ideal. It means you can get away from the family, close the door and make your phone calls. It means you can get yourself organised. Making sales of any product always involves paperwork. Having customers, always involves records and administration. Party plan usually involves credit cards — mainly yours and it's advisable to have a specific credit card and a specific bank account for your business. Keeping track always involves systems, paperwork, administration, files and being organised. At the very least, have a folder with all your orders in it. So if someone wants to return something, or if someone asks you when their order is likely to arrive, you can quite easily find the relevant information.

Have a box, one of the plastic ones on wheels and a lid is ideal, set up to carry your party plan tools — order forms, pens, catalogues, recruitment brochures, hostess kits, diary for bookings, to name just a few. And the day after each party, go through it and restock it. Ensure you are never short on order forms or catalogues. Always have more than you think you need, and when you get low, order more immediately.

You will need to keep copies of all transactions through your credit card and bank account. Keep accurate track of cash transactions. You will need to keep track of what dates payments are going to come out of either your credit card or your bank account to pay for your orders, and you will need to keep track of what you have put into this card or account, so you are keeping track of your expenses. Otherwise you can get into a real mess and end up paying extra bank fees (usually about $40 a day for overdrawn accounts and/or fees for going over the limit on your credit card. Banks don't refuse to pay once you go over the limit on your credit card, they allow it and sting you in fees for the privilege. Keeping track can save you a lot of money!

A trap for new players is that they don't keep track of their expenses. They purchase stands and a number of display items, which will display the products better or complement the display. They buy new stock and spend their bonus gifts on things they'd like for themselves rather than on product they can sell and make more profit on. And they don't keep track of what they are spending or how much money they are making — or not as the case may be.

Remember, if you get offered free gifts because of the size of your order, then purchase popular products, which you can make more profit on. If you sell something which you haven't had to pay for, that is called 100% PROFIT! You not only want to feel good doing this business, you want it to be profitable. And many people use their stock as if it was their own. They give away pieces, they give bigger discounts than necessary and they buy what they want, rather than what they think they can sell more of.

NOTES

NOTES

5

Business, The Great Teacher

Sarah's first party was behind her when she and Jenny next met. So Jenny was keen to discuss what she'd done and where they could both improve. Jenny was eager to talk about the future and the success of their next parties. Sarah, however, wasn't so enthusiastic. Her party had been disappointing. Ten had been invited and only four had turned up. "I don't know if this is the right thing for me," she told Jenny. "It's all a bit disappointing really. And Jeff is totally unimpressed with the money I've spent so far."

"Well, let's have a look at what might have happened." Jenny was undeterred. "How did your hostess coaching go?" she asked.

"What do you mean, when I booked the party?" Sarah asked, puzzled.

"No, you know — hostess coaching. Where you keep in touch with her. You encourage her to show the catalogue around and, if people can't attend, get her to take orders. External orders can really increase the sales of a party. If you give her an incentive to have good sales, she'll usually try and get good sales. WIIFM — remember? What's In It For Me? The customer is always interested in how it's going to work better for her. You always have to give her a reason to do things for you."

"God, you're starting to sound like Sandra." Sarah sipped her coffee.

"Yeah, that's because what she tells us works!" Jenny leaned forward. "Look Sarah, why did you join? What did you want to get from this?"

"Good question. I've been wondering myself," Sarah answered despondently.

Jenny looked at her, concern in her voice. " Sarah, didn't you want to go to conference? Hawaii? Remember? Where have you got a picture of what you want?"

"What do you mean? A picture of Hawaii?"

" A vision board or a journal. Anywhere you can look and see what you want. I've got a fake cheque on my vision board for $1300 a month income.

That's what I'm going to earn and that's what I see on my vision board every time I walk into my office."

"What office?" Sarah frowned.

"I've converted my spare room into an office. It's great! I'm learning to keep track and that's really inspiring for me. I know exactly where everything is, but more importantly, I know where I stand. Come and see."

Sarah was impressed. The spare room had transformed into a tidy business-like office. There was a desk, shelves, filing cabinet and a large cork board with a range of pictures on it — Jenny's vision board. Her diary was open on the desk and Sarah noticed that not only were parties booked in, she had blocks of time set aside for hostess coaching and follow-up calls. Boxes of stock were stacked neatly in what had been a wardrobe and her party box was in the middle of the floor, with the lid on the floor beside it. "I was just re-ordering when you arrived," Jenny said. "Stocking my party box with more order forms and catalogues," she explained as if it was a bit messy. "Let's sit down and review our parties and see if there's anything we can spot which we could do better in the future. I suspect that there are some crucial ingredients to a successful party," suggested Jenny.

Sarah agreed and Jenny was delighted to see a spark of energy in her friend and that Sarah's enthusiasm was coming back.

"So firstly, I did three hostess coaching calls and my hostess got some outside orders. Not a lot, but it increased her overall sales so she was able to afford to buy the bag-and-shoe set she really lusted for. Every time I called, we talked about her shoes and her bag." Jenny giggled. "It got so as I wouldn't mind having the set myself. She was starting to sell me on them, as well!"

"How did you know what products she wanted?" asked Sarah.

"At the party she came to, she put it on her wish list. When I went to talk to her, she was admiring it in the brochure. So every time I spoke to her, we talked about that set. It's exactly the same as us focusing on our goals. Give her a goal she really wants and she'll try to have more people at the party and will try to sell a bit more. And I don't mean being pushy," Jenny anticipated Sarah's objection. "I mean that if you're enthusiastic, you will get more people attending and buying more."

Sarah admitted she hadn't done any hostess coaching other than booking the party and phoning the week before to confirm that everything was booked. "Wouldn't three calls be a bit of a nuisance?" Sarah suggested doubtfully. "That would be a bit much for me, I'd get a bit sick of someone calling all the time."

"Not if you felt that they were friendly calls. The first one is two weeks before to encourage her to pass around the catalogue and to urge her on to get at least 10 invitations out there. The second one was a week before and the suggestion was to get her to follow up, confirm people's attendance and see if she has picked up any orders from her catalogues. And the third was two days before the party to see if there's anything she's worried about and reassure her if need be. And again to encourage her to follow up on her external sales. Ingredient number one is Hostess Coaching," declared Jenny.

"But," Sarah had a problem. "That was a really busy time for me. I can't see how I would have had the time."

Jenny shook her head. "That's what I thought. But I gave up my TV two nights a week and made a few phone calls instead. I booked them into my diary and I shut myself away in my office and made those calls. To begin with, it was hard to do but it felt so good when they were done. My energy and self-confidence just grew."

Sarah made another note in the notebook she had brought with her.

Ingredient Number 1 — Hostess Coaching
Self-discipline required — create the time to do it

Sarah sighed. "Now I come to think about it, I didn't have enough catalogues either. I can see how if each person has her own catalogue, that gives everyone plenty more time to browse. I thought it would be okay if they shared. You know, save me the cost of ordering more."

"If they browse, they have more time to build a wish list," added Jenny. "You want them to want something, badly."

Ingredient Number 2 — Be prepared
Self-discipline required — get organised

They discussed the aspects of displaying the products and discovered that they both did a great job in display and presentation of the shoes and bags. The fact that they both loved them seemed to lead naturally to displaying them well.

"You know what I think? When we started, we thought that it was the display that makes the sales. But I'm starting to think that while the display is important, there are so many other things which are as important, if not vital." Sarah was pleased with herself. Looking back at the parties, was a helpful exercise. It was getting her refocused and her energy and enthusiasm were back in spades.

"I agree. But I still think the display is important as that's what they look at when they arrive. That's what drives them to pore through the catalogue. That's what makes them want something. So it's important to find good ways of displaying the products." This was something they both agreed on.

Ingredient Number 3 — Learn display skills to show
the product at its best

"How did you start your party?" asked Jenny. "I learned the script that Jenny gave me but I know I missed bits. I felt a bit of a goose and it didn't really feel natural. But it seemed to me, that when I'd finished, they just started buying."

Again Sarah looked rueful. "I didn't have time to learn the script so I just told them a bit about the company and then let them look at the product."

"But didn't you tell them a bit about yourself and why you'd joined?"

Sarah shook her head. "No, I don't feel comfortable talking about myself. I don't see the need for it."

Jenny looked thoughtful. "I figured that Sandra knew what worked so I just learned it. I didn't feel that good about it, but something worked at my last party. I could feel it. And I suspect that the script was a part of it. You know, there are some people out there who are earning a fabulous living through party plan. They have tried different things and found what works. I guess it's no different from learning anything else. Learn how to do it and you get better results. I'm going to make a real effort and learn it off by heart."

Sarah could see that Jenny was determined to make her business work. But she was not sure that she could ever feel good about following a script. However, she made a note in her notebook to read through the script and see if there was anything in there which she could try or adapt to what was comfortable for her to say.

Ingredient Number 4 — What you say when you open the party
Self-discipline required — being prepared to step
outside of your comfort zone to learn something new

"You know it seems to me that holding a successful party is about more things than I originally thought," Jenny suggested. "When we watched Sandra, I thought it was all to do with her confidence and what she was saying. I still think that confidence is important, but I think there's more to a successful party than I originally thought."

"That's probably why it takes a while to be consistently successful," Sarah continued. "You learn some things and get some things right and you get sales. But there are other things that you have to learn as well. Some parties will not go well because of the things we haven't learned yet." Sarah was pleased with this observation. This session with Jenny made her feel renewed again. She was looking forward to her next party, which was at the end of the week.

"You know," Jenny seemed far away, "now I stop and think about it, the people who came late, turned up either during or after my presentation. They didn't buy like the others who heard the whole thing. They were polite but weren't focused on me or the products. They chatted to each other more and were less interested. I think our opening presentation is so much more vital than I ever thought. Perhaps, there are several things which are more important than we originally thought," Jenny added.

"You know," Sarah stood up. "I'm going to cut this session short. I'm going home to do some Hostess Coaching. And not just the lady for the end of this week. I'm going to call my hostesses for next week as well. And I've got to order some more catalogues and order forms," Sarah added over her shoulder as she headed out the door.

Jenny continued to sit at the table sipping coffee. She flipped through her diary, looking at the weeks ahead and the dates she had parties booked in. She started to enter Hostess Coaching into her diary. She knew what days she wouldn't have a hope, when the kids' needs swamped everything else in her life. So some weeks, she put the Hostess Coaching a bit earlier in the week as she recognised that she wouldn't realistically get much of a chance. But now that she realised how vital Hostess Coaching was, she wasn't going to let herself down by not doing it. She was going to learn and practise her presentation until she was polished and natural. She could be herself while using a guide, a script to get the best results. Again, she wasn't going to let herself down by not doing it well. She smiled. That sounded good. And it also sounded like something that would get her to a $1,300 a month income. While she was at it, Jenny reviewed her goals and spent a bit of time dreaming what it would be like. Once we have caught up on the bills, what will we spend the money on, she wondered. She'd actually not thought past that. She started to make a list of all the things she would spend the money on once they had cleared the bills. First, there was the bills they were behind on, then the credit cards, her Myer card and then came a list of things for the kids. Wow, maybe they could afford a great family holiday next year. Jenny took her list and pinned it to her vision board. She was going to tick all those things off one at a time. She sat down and reminded herself how many sales she needed in order to earn her $1,300 a month. It seemed like a lot. So she broke it down into parties. If she had three parties a week, suddenly it became quite manageable. Jenny checked her figures. It absolutely was achievable. In fact, if she booked a few more parties into her month, she could easily exceed that! To say Jenny was surprised was an understatement. She thought it would require much more than that.

Later that night after the kids had gone to bed, she went over the figures again with Mark. "Could that be right?" she asked him as he hammered away at the calculator.

"Hang on a minute, I want to show you something," he said. She knew he was excited, she could hear it in his voice. "Let's say you do three parties a week, which is absolutely possible," he said. "One during the week and two in the weekend. You could fit that in easy. In fact, I think you should be aiming for four a week until you get a team up and running."

"Easy for you to say," Jenny laughed. "I've got to get the bookings first."

"Okay, let's work with three parties a week, 12 a month. Now," he was tapping away at the calculator again. "And if we add what your average sales are per party, let's take the average so we're being conservative, no… let's throw in a few small ones to make this realistic and achievable. And here's your potential revenue for the month. My god, I think you better forget about your target. You're aiming too low."

"What do you mean?" Jenny was lost.

Mark laughed. "Ta Da! $2,520! Forget your target, you'd better raise your sights."

"Yes!" Jenny couldn't believe her ears. And then she realised. "Hawaii here we come! Are you sure that's correct?" She pored over the brochure. "I think I can really do this. I mean, really do this. For a beginner, I'm going really well. What will I be doing when I get good at it?"

"Let's take a look," suggested Mark.

"I don't know if that's a good idea," objected Jenny. "Isn't that a bit like tempting fate?"

"You women!" Mark frowned. "How are you going to set new targets if you're not looking at the real picture? How can you plan? How can you motivate yourself if you're aiming too low?"

"But what if I aim high and miss it? What if I start aiming too high?"

Mark sat back and looked at her. "Will you listen to yourself? You sound like Sarah. Listen you, this is my trip to Hawaii you're messing with here. Let's aim high. What've we got to lose?"

Jenny smiled. A small, self-satisfied smile. "So when did it become 'we'?"

"All right, I was a bit of a schmuck to begin with. But I saw the light, didn't I? I mean $2,520 a month is enough for anyone to see the light. Let's go further." He grabbed the calculator and pulled the brochure towards him. "If you had three people in your team, doing much less each party than what you would usually do, look at what you'd be earning." He turned the calculator for her to see the total.

"Are you kidding me? Are you sure you haven't made a mistake? Is that a month?" Jenny was breathless. "Are you sure? " she whispered.

Mark nodded and looked triumphant. "I'm sure, babe. I think you should start to focus on recruiting. There's some serious money to be made.

And with a team, you're not out doing all the parties, you just have to train them up in what you're already good at. I mean, the one sure way to find out if this is achievable is to try and do it."

Jenny stared at the new total. "Wow! I've got to learn how to grow a team."

6

Coaching For A Successful Business

Business is a great teacher. It will reflect back to you what you are good at and what you need to learn to do better. It will challenge you, delightfully (not) enlighten you on your comfort zones and it will show you how strong or weak your goals are. Because as soon as you have to do something new or different, your emotional reaction will be to justify why you shouldn't have to do it the new way. Some examples of a comfort zone being threatened are:

- You will tell yourself you haven't the time.
- You will say that it doesn't feel right to you.
- You will point out that's not what you would normally say.

And how you respond to these excuses, will indicate your future success or lack of it in your business. You will either face your discomfort and work your way through it. or you will use your discomfort as an excuse to walk away.

You will either face your discomfort and work your way through it or you will use your discomfort as an excuse to walk away.

It's not really right for me.
I don't think I'm cut out to do this.
It's not the right time.

Firstly let me say this, nothing is good or bad, but everything has consequences. Successful people before you have tried a range of strategies and know what works and why it works. To begin with, they will simply explain to you what to do that works. In our infinite wisdom, we decide that what we have been told by an expert who has proven they know what they are talking about, is not the right thing for us. If you can relate to this, then understand that really what is happening is simply this. A part of you, let's call her Madge, is fearful of trying something new. Madge does not like you being out of your comfort zone and feeling vulnerable. Madge is terrified that if you try something new, you'll fail and you'll look stupid. And Madge has been well trained. At school, you were rewarded for not making mistakes. This training runs deep. As a teenager, you were petrified of looking stupid or not being one of the crowd. Or you might have been one of those rebels who did the opposite of what you were told.

Regardless of which background you had, we have an ingrained fear of failure and of feeling vulnerable. If you wish to go deeper into this, read my book, **Coach Yourself to Wealth**. It is this very fear that keeps us short of money. Madge stops us pursuing our dreams. But most tragically of all, she stops us achieving our full potential.

But there are two pieces of good news here! Firstly, if you challenge Madge, she weakens. The more you push against your boundaries and face your fears, the more you demonstrate to her that you are bigger than your fears. She weakens, you become stronger. So I say, DOWN WITH MADGE!!

The other piece of good news is that party plan is an industry that encourages you to make mistakes. It is such a big world of customers out there, that if you have a party that doesn't live up to your expectations and is a flop, there are plenty more potential customers out there to practise on. Becoming successful in party plan is all about giving something a try, and then getting better at it. But it involves action. If you just keep the activities high, you will break through.

So the ideal attitude is to surge ahead, don't worry if you think you might make a mistake; don't worry if you think that people mightn't like you; don't worry if you think you are going to make a fool of yourself — that's just Madge speaking. The reality is that in the very fact that you are running this party, you already have the admiration of most people in the room. Remember when you looked at someone doing that and said: "I couldn't do that." Well, they don't know what you are supposed or not supposed to say and do. So it's just Madge nibbling away at your courage, undermining your confidence in yourself. DOWN WITH MADGE!! The best way to push through your fears is to refocus on your goals.

The best way to push through your fears is to refocus on your goals.

This is why your goals are so important. As soon as Madge starts the What if... you need to go back and refocus on your goals. When you make a mistake (yes, you are moving forward!) refocus on your goals. When you are not looking at your goals, you will see problems. When you are focused on your goals, you ask yourself a completely different set of questions. Your success depends upon the quality of questions you ask yourself.

Not — I can't do this. But — How can I learn to do this?

Not — I don't feel good about this. But — How can I learn to feel better about this?

Your brain will find answers for you and if you ask the right questions, it will feed you helpful suggestions. You'll suddenly get a good idea, or you'll suddenly think about someone who would be the ideal person to ask. Ask the right questions and you don't focus on what you don't know, you focus on finding a way forward. The formula for success is simply learn something new, take action, make mistakes, re-learn and correct and repeat the above. Over and over again.

The formula for success is simply learn something new, take action, make mistakes, re-learn and correct and repeat the above. Over and over again.

The Recipe For Party Plan Success

Ingredient 1 — Hostess Coaching

There's no doubt that your hostess can make or break your party. I remember a party I did, where the hostess opened the party by telling everyone about a previous party of mine she'd been to. She gave me a glowing reference and told them all how good she thought I was. She then described with great gusts of laughter, how bad another lady had been at a previous party she'd attended and how she had tried to get each of them to have a party as well. She absolutely blew out the window any chance I had of getting any further party bookings. I couldn't believe what I was hearing and I'd had such hope of this particular group of women. So, I set myself a target of absolutely getting at least one party booking from this group. And I did. So it is important that you don't assume that your hostess knows what to do to make a successful party for you both. She doesn't know what works and what increases sales so you have to coach her.

Firstly, find out why she agreed to have the party. What is it she wants to get? Most likely she wants some of the products at half price or for free. If so, it's vital that you know specifically what product she wants, as you need to keep talking about it to motivate her to do some extra things around arranging the party. And don't be surprised if what she wants is really quite small and inexpensive. People love getting stuff for free or for half price — even when they could quite easily afford to buy it outright. We all love getting a bargain or, even better, something for free. And if it's something of good quality, so much the better. Better to boast to your friends about. And that's exactly what you want to have happen.

Firstly, you want her to invite approximately 10 people, so make sure that she has several catalogues well before the party. If she shows it to people when she invites them, they will more than likely find something they want and this will motivate them to come to the party and not drop out at the last minute. Secondly, if they can't come to the party, encourage her to leave a catalogue with them so they can shop through it and purchase even if they aren't going to attend the party. So encourage her to pass the catalogue around and get as many pre-party sales as possible. It can send your sales figures through the roof if you have orders from those who can't attend at each party you do.

Teach her how to talk about the party. Why should her friends, who will be tired at the end of the day, make an effort to tidy themselves up and get to her place? Sometimes, the attraction is getting together with the girls; sometimes it's getting out of the house; it's getting away from hubby and the kids for a bit; it's having a glass of wine and chatting with other women; and sometimes, if you're lucky, it's because they've seen the product and they want to buy. Sometimes it's because they've seen the product and they can't afford to buy, but it's still fun trying it all on. But she has to invite them in a way that tempts them so they want to come along. Give her a few phrases to say to her friends.

Guide her through the process of preparing for and running the party. Where are you going to hold it? What time do you want everyone there and what time are you going to start? How long is your presentation going to be? What is she going to serve? Tea, coffee and biscuits or wine and nibbles? And when is she going to serve it, before, during or after the presentation?

You see, all these things either increase your sales or reduce them. If she starts pouring wine and handing out nibbles while you're doing your presentation, you'll lose their attention and you'll get fewer sales. So you need at least a couple of hostess calls, either phone or face to face. Plus you'll need a call the week before. So, when someone books a party, immediately book into your diary your Hostess Coaching calls. That way you won't get overwhelmed if you get busy. It will just pop up in your diary.

Plus, when you have finished the party, here's a tip which some very successful party plan ladies have passed on to me. Rebook your hostess for her next party. They simply pick up their diary, and ask: "When can I pencil you in for your next party?" Some hostesses would surprise by booking their next party as close as two to six weeks. Others would book further out, but the main thing is, many simply pencil in a new booking.

You can also start a hostess loyalty club. If you find that on average, your hostesses usually book two parties a year, create a loyalty club where if they hold three parties a year, they get an extra 10% off each party to spend at the third party. So they don't actually get the benefit until the third party. Just imagine for a moment, if every one of your hostesses did two parties a year. And then imagine if they all did three parties a year. You would start each month off with parties already booked in your diary. Way to go!

Remember, offer the free dates in your diary for parties within the next three to four weeks. Don't leave it for them to choose. And never simply ask: "When would you like your party?" Do not accept parties past four weeks until your diary is fully booked. Then and only then, will you accept parties past that date. In reality, the further out the parties are booked, the more likely it is that they will get cancelled or postponed. Time can weaken the reason why they originally decided to hold the party.

Preparation Is Like A Dinner Party

Many people. when they first start party plan, see the party as being the main thing which happens which contributes to their sales. They grab everything they need at the last minute as they race out the door and expect to do great sales. But party plan is exactly the same as planning a dinner party. You've probably never really thought about what goes into a dinner party, but stop and think about it for a moment. You decide to hold a dinner party. First you have to decide on the date. And that may change as you find out that some of the main people you want there, are unable to attend. Often, you will have a special reason why you are having the dinner party, or you may decide to run with a theme. Or maybe it's just a great excuse to get everyone together that you haven't seen for a while.

Secondly, you have to decide upon the menu. Dinner or barbeque? What are you going to have for pre-dinner nibbles? How formal the dinner is, will dictate whether you have chips and snacks, or antipasto. What are you going to have for a main course? Dessert? Coffee and cheese or fruit or chocolates? What wine and drinks will you need?

Once your menu is decided upon, you can decide what drinks to have before, during and after the meal. Now you go shopping. You have to buy all the ingredients for the dinner plus all the drinks and nibbles. While you're at it, you'll probably buy something to make the table look great. A new table cloth or new place mats, candles or you might even splash out on new glasses, cutlery or a new dinner set.

Next comes the cooking and preparation. You need to organise yourself so you have time to prepare everything. And you either love this part of the process or it's something you have to do to have a great dinner party. Once every thing is prepared, you have to set the scene. You may set the table and arrange the room. You might have brought fresh flowers or you might move some furniture and remove some clutter.

And last but not least, you prepare yourself for the dinner party. Shower, clothes, make-up, jewellery. And you're ready. The food's ready, the table is ready and you're ready to greet the guests and ensure the dinner party runs smoothly with everyone enjoying themselves, including you.

But all anyone else will see, is the actual dinner party. Some of them will wonder how you do it. You're such a busy person and this dinner party looks effortless. You seem elegant and unstressed as a hostess. But what they don't see, is all the preparation that resulted in the dinner party.

And it's the same with party plan. The party is the end result of all the preparation you have done before. We look at experienced party plan people and wonder how their parties can be so successful. We wonder how they manage to get so many bookings. And most of all, we wonder how they get to be so good at recruiting. Well, the successful party is the end result of many things behind the scenes. And when I talk about a successful party, I mean one that achieves or exceeds your sales goals, which leads to at least two to three more party bookings, and one which leads to at least one recruitment.

A successful party is one that achieves or exceeds your sales goals, which leads to at least two to three more party bookings and leads to at least one recruitment.

These should be your goals at every party you run. These should be your focus for everything you do prior to the party, during the party and after the party.

So, what is your preparation you should be doing before the party? The most basic thing is to set the goals you wish to achieve at every party. This may mean that you go back and identify how much money you want to make each month. You may be aiming for conference, you may be aiming at a certain level within the company or you may have revenue goals. Set your goals first.

Secondly, you have to get on the phone and start phoning to make bookings. This means you need to think about what you are going to say and what is the most successful thing to say. And you need to practise it out loud before you start calling.

You need to be actively using your diary. Planning what time you have available for parties. Booking in phoning time, whether that be for booking parties or for Hostess Coaching. You need to make sure you always have enough stationary, such as order forms, catalogues, pens etc in your party box.

Next, you have to plan your party. How are you going to get increased sales? These things don't happen. Everything you do has consequences. Learn your script and give your presentation where you cover everything in the right order. A good presentation contains three bids for bookings, three bids for recruitment and a call to action. This way you will get more bookings and more nibbles for information on the business. Go your own way, saying what you think is right, and your sales will be lower, you won't get as many bookings and very little recruitment.

Implement many strategies to increase your sales and you will see your sales soar.

Ensure that you are well-groomed, have great energy and are passionate about your business. People love being around passionate people and your sales, bookings and recruitment will all grow. If you are organised, focused, enthusiastic, prepared and professional, you will grow your business. But this does not happen by accident. You may grow your sales for a while, but if you are not consciously doing all these things, firstly you will plateau and secondly, if and when you grow your team, you won't be an effective leader or teacher. The party sales are the consequence of everything you do prior to, and during, the party.

If you are organised, focused, enthusiastic, prepared and professional, you will grow your business. Party sales are the consequence of what you do prior to and during the party.

Your Presentation — The First Emotional Connection

I want you to think for a moment about the last time you bought something you wanted. You would have looked at it, imagined owning it and imagined how owning it would make you look and feel. Then you would have thought through all the reasons why this would be a good idea for you to have it. It is important for you to understand that there are two processes happening here, which happen every time someone buys something.

Firstly, there is the Emotional Connection to the item you want to buy. And that is exactly what an Emotional Connection is — you want it. You need it, you must have it. You desire it. The second part of the process is the logical process, which goes with this. You justify why you should have it — the reasons behind this purchase. And the logical process is usually driven by the Emotional Connection. You want it so you find plenty of reasons to back up this desire. Without the Emotional Connection, you will think it would be nice to have, but don't have enough motivation to take action.

**Firstly, there is the Emotional Connection to the thing you
want to buy.
You desire it, you must have it.
The second part of the process is the logical process,
which goes with this.
You justify why you should have it.
Without the Emotional Connection, you think it would be
nice to have but don't have enough motivation to take action.**

Watch the ladies at your parties and listen to what they say. They look at a product, they want it. They admire it and, if you've been clever, they will be touching and holding it. They are imagining wearing or using it. Now the logical process kicks in to back up the Emotional Connection. They start telling themselves or the person next to them, why this would be a good idea for them to get. They explain what it will go with, how they are going to use it or where they are going to wear it. This is the logic backing up the Emotional Connection.

And every time you strengthen that Emotional Connection at your parties, you increase your sales, your bookings and your recruiting.

A successful presentation at the start of a party, creates an Emotional Connection firstly to you, secondly to your company and lastly to your products. That is why if anyone arrives late, after your presentation, you can almost guarantee that they won't buy as much as the others who heard the whole presentation. Unless, of course, they came to the party to buy a specific product.

**A successful presentation at the start of a party,
creates an Emotional Connection firstly to you,
secondly to your company
and lastly to your products.**

Why to you first? If your group can relate to you as a woman and mother with the same problems and challenges that they have, you will inspire them and touch them. Quite simply, they will make an Emotional Connection with you. This means that they will share your enthusiasm, they will trust you and open up to you and not only share what they want, but what obstacles they have in buying it. They will want to buy from you. This is a very powerful technique, which will not only increase your sales, but plants a seed for those women who have similar situations to you, to start to consider the idea of getting into the business.

Secondly, talking about your company, it's history, how it started and what good things it's doing for both its hostesses and its consultants, creates a sense of security and loyalty that this is a company they want to buy from. They 'd love to work for a company that offers these kinds of rewards for its consultants.

Thirdly, talking about the product, gives them knowledge, which enables them to complete the logical part of the sale. They will need this to justify both to themselves and their partners as to why they want to spend this much money on these products. But painting a picture of what impact this will have, is creating the Emotional Connection. That means that you will not have to sell it, they will want to buy it — the best situation to be in.

Creating the Emotional Connection to the product means that you will not have to sell it, they will want to buy it.

Action

Learn your script for your presentation at the party off by heart and out loud — over and over again until you are completely comfortable saying it, and will therefore deliver it completely naturally.

Try and read as many self-development books or listen to CDs to keep you motivated and focused.

NOTES

NOTES

NOTES

7

The Secret Behind Successful Bookings

At her next party, Jenny was much more relaxed about her presentation. She was more natural and was easily able to focus on creating an Emotional Connection to herself, the company and the products. She found she was involving the women more, asking them questions, which built upon what she was saying. She was able to add a bit of humour and was delighted to see, that at the end of her presentation, many people were immediately ready to order. Others were picking up the shoes, opening the bags and trying them over their shoulders, and she could hear the logical process in full swing. Her hostess had orders from people she had shown the catalogue to, and as she now listened much more carefully to people's comments, the thing she used to dread — "I can't afford it", or "I don't have any money", Jenny now saw as an invitation to talk about the hostess rewards. In fact, if anyone really wanted one of the top-of-the-range items, she would encourage them to have her own party to get a great deal. Her hostess had responded well to Jenny's coaching and eight people turned up for the party. Good numbers of attendees, higher sales than she'd had before and Jenny got three bookings and one inquiry about joining the business. She was ecstatic! She couldn't wait to get home and tell Mark.

Sarah had had a party that night also. The next day when they talked on the phone, Sarah had reasonable sales but only one booking and no recruitment interest.

"How did your presentation go?" asked Jenny, now keen to identify what might inhibit the sales. "Had you spent some time learning it?"

Sarah hesitated. "I read through it, but it's just not me to say those things." She sounded a bit down and frustrated.

"So, what did you decide to say? Did you re-word it a bit so you felt more comfortable? And then learn it?"

"No, I ran out of time. So I just had a mental note of what I had to cover. And my sales weren't that bad. It's not as if I didn't do any sales."

No, thought Jenny, but I suspect you could have done a lot better. She was starting to realise that Sarah was nowhere as motivated as she was. And she was a bit puzzled as how to find the trigger to keep her motivated. It was almost as if Sarah was deliberately putting obstacles in her own way to stop her doing well. Jenny didn't understand this at all. You either want to do it and give it 100 percent or you don't do it as far as she was concerned.

"Besides," Sarah added, "Jeff is not happy with the money I'm spending. And he's getting a bit sick of babysitting while I go out to 'party' as he calls it. I don't know if this is going to work for me, really," she sighed.

"Did you do the family session? That worked a treat for us. The family's great. Sinead has even started doing the evening dishes so I can get ready earlier. Wonders never cease!" she chuckled. "If you'd have told me that a month ago, I would never have believed it. But our family meeting really got them to see my vision. Have you done one?" Jenny insisted.

"Look Jenny," Sarah sounded a bit defensive. "It's all right for you but my family is different. We've never done that sort of thing before. I'd feel a bit stupid suggesting it. They'd probably not want to agree to it anyway, knowing them."

Jenny was suddenly hit with the realisation that Sarah wasn't prepared to push through anything which made her feel uncomfortable, and gave one last try.

"But Sarah, these are the things which help make your business work, the script and the family meeting. Why don't you just give it a try?"

There was a short silence. "Yeah. I'll have a think about it tomorrow. Look, I've got to go now. I'll call you later."

Jenny sat for a while thinking this through. True, it had been Jenny who had been the most keen to join, but Sarah had seemed motivated to make a go of it. Jenny was faced with a choice, she could either spend time and energy on trying to get Sarah on her way, or she could put her focus on her own business and encourage Sarah whenever she got the opportunity. Logic said the second choice, but Jenny had a strange sense of abandoning her. What was a friendship meant to be about if when one faltered, you simply walked away? Jenny didn't feel right about it, but she had a strange feeling that she was missing something. She imagined doing the business without her discussions with Sarah, and was engulfed with a feeling of loneliness. Surely, there was something she could do! If I can do it, Sarah can too.

However, she was so disturbed about the whole situation, that she brought it up with Mark that night after the kids were in bed. "I know she can do it, it seems like she wants to. She's just not doing the action she needs to take to make it work." Jenny felt genuinely miserable about her friend.

"Maybe that's not the issue," suggested Mark.

"What do you mean?"

"Well, she can do it, but there must be a lot of other factors which dictate success. We're all capable of doing things, but there has to be a motivation to get us past our excuses. As Paula, a good friend of mine always says: 'You can have lots of reasons not to do something, but it only takes one good reason to do it.' We have to have a reason to drive us to push past being comfortable. Not everyone has that motivation. You've got it in spades, but I don't think Sarah has it. I've never thought Sarah has had it. She's always made excuses, she's a real wishful thinker but she's not prepared to do anything about it. She just complains. You've always been the one who leads the two of you into things. I've always thought that about her, but she was your friend so I wasn't going to say anything."

"Wow! Fancy you seeing that and me not noticing."

"You had no reason to until now. I think that what you should do is to encourage her any chance you get, but put your focus on growing your own business. You're growing, she's not. You have to realise that as you grow and develop, you leave friends behind who don't want to go on that journey with you. And that's okay, too."

Surprised, Jenny digested what Mark had said. Then she grinned, leaned forward and gave him a kiss on the lips. "When did you get so wise?"

He tried to look modest, failing miserably. "Why don't we have a look and see why you got so many bookings this time?"

Jenny felt warm and fully supported. Was this something the two of them could truly work on together? That would be a true partnership. She loved the idea.

"So, the three ladies who made the bookings, why did they book?" continued Mark.

Jenny thought for a moment. "Well, two of them really, really wanted a shoe-and-bag set and thought the hostess offer was great. The third couldn't afford to buy what she wanted, and so she had the party 'cos she could get it half price."

"Okay," said Mark. "So what about the others who wanted bags. Why didn't they have a party?"

"Well, as you know, some of them just bought what they wanted. It didn't seem to be a problem price-wise. Others weren't keen enough to either buy or book." She looked at Mark, the answer dawning on her face. "They didn't make an Emotional Connection to the shoes or the bags! Those who had made a strong Emotional Connection to either the bags or the shoes had money as a barrier. And the answer was to have their own party!" She thought for a moment. "You know, I noticed at one stage that there was a small group of people who couldn't keep their hands off the bags. They were picking them up, slinging them over their shoulder. They were turning them over, opening them up and one lady even tried putting all her stuff from her bag into the new one to see if it fitted."

"And?" Mark couldn't see where this was leading.

"All those ladies who were touching the bags, some even stroking them, were the ones who either bought, or had a party. Most of those who didn't buy, sat flicking through the catalogue. I wonder what would have happened if I had zeroed in on them and worked through the range until I found something they liked? And got them to handle them, to touch them."

"But surely it makes more sense to spend time with the ones who already want to buy. I mean, you don't have a lot of time, do you?"

"No, but I wonder if when I have finished collecting my orders, or when someone is trying to make a decision, if I approached someone I thought had potential..."

"Who on earth is someone with potential?" Mark demanded. "Don't they all have potential?" he asked.

Jenny smiled. "I figured out that those who are already wearing smart shoes, or carrying a great bag, are far easier to sell to because they already have a weakness for them. Do you know what I think?" Jenny was trying to think things through logically. "I think that maybe I can allocate my time more effectively. If I can spread myself a bit further, maybe I can make more sales. After all, I suspect I'm the reason some sales happen."

"So, what are you going to do? Pick the people who are ready to sell first and then go to the others, but pick the ones with the most potential after the first round of orders?"

"No, I think that if someone is ready to buy, I take their order, try to up-sell, plant the idea of a party and move on. In fact, they already have the form about joining the business to lean on. I'll see if I can laminate some fliers on having a party as well. Anyway, I'll talk to them again later because I've started phoning all the people who placed an order to see if they're happy with their order, and to see if I can tempt them to have their own party. So I don't have to spend a lot of time with them on the night. Enough for them to feel looked after, but then move on to others. Until now, I have spent as much time with all those who aren't buying as those who did, but maybe I'll approach those with potential first. Although, I don't want to fall into the trap of making assumptions. I'm fast learning that you can't pick who is interested in having a party and who's not. Still it would be good to maximise my time when there was a large number of people at the party."

"What do you mean, up-sell?" Mark wasn't familiar with the term.

"Well, when someone buys something, the big decision is, shall I buy it or not? That's the big one. That's the one people agonise over and this is when the logical part of the sale is most used, when someone is trying to make the big decision. And the fact of the matter is, some people just can't make decisions quickly. However, once they have decided to buy, buying a bit more is painless. Think about buying a car. You spend so much time looking, thinking, doing your figures and working out, should I or shouldn't I? Then when you finally make the decision, you also get tinted windows, mats for the inside and the boot, etc. See what I mean?"

Mark grinned. "You're right! That's why they walk you through the checklist after you've bought the car. Because buying extras is nothing after you've made the decision to buy. Well, I'll be damned. And with women, when you buy a dress, you usually want to buy shoes or jewellery to go with it. Maybe a belt or scarf? Right. So how does this work for you?"

"Well, you can increase your sales significantly by adding value or up-selling. Say, for example, a woman loves a pair of shoes and decides to buy them. She's looked at them, compared them mentally with what she's seen in the shops and she's spent some time walking around the room and admiring them in the mirror. Yes, she's going to buy them. So then I ask her, have you seen the bag, which goes with these? She may be hesitant, but I tell her that if she buys the shoe set, which is the bag and the shoes, she'll be saving $X on them. Individually, they are almost twice what she would be paying for them. And because she has already decided to buy, making this extra decision is easy. And then, of course, I suggest she buy the wallet to go with the bag. Most people who buy the bag will buy the wallet to go with it. It's getting so that it's seldom that a person just buys a pair of shoes at my parties. I always manage to up-sell something. To me, it just seems the logical thing to do, I mean, why would you buy a bag and not buy the wallet to go with it?"

"So that's why you get such good sales at your parties! That's why your average party sales are higher than most. It's not because you have more people at the parties, it's because you up-sell and add value." Mark was surprised, He didn't realise you could influence people to that degree to tempt them to buy more.

"Well, that and I encourage my hostesses to get outside orders. What I'm finding, is that when someone says they can't come to the party, once they see the catalogue, many of them find they can come after all. It will be interesting to see what happens in the second round of parties with my hostesses. I don't think they'll have so much trouble getting people to come along once they have bought something or seen the catalogue."

Mark pushed further. "So, back to the all-important bookings. Why didn't you get so many bookings at your last party?"

Jenny thought out loud. "What did I do differently this time? After the presentation, I spoke to each person. Last time, I was a bit flustered and I only spoke to the people who obviously wanted to order. This time I was listening much harder to what they were saying. I was looking for the clues which would enable me to talk about the hostess gifts."

"So, does that mean that every person who books a party does it to get either a particular pair of shoes or a specific bag?" Mark pressed again.

"Well, I didn't. I had a party because I was interested in getting into the business. But I think it would be a good idea to take note why each person agrees to have a party. Bookings are vital to growing my business. Sandra told me that if I was serious about growing a business, not to fall into the trap of just focusing on sales. She said that when some people start, they are so delighted with the sales they make, that they run out of parties. You have to focus on bookings to grow the business. That's why I'm making such a big deal about it."

"What do you mean, run out of parties?" Mark was confused.

"Well, you get started by asking your friends and family to have a party for you. At each party, you will have some people you don't know. What you want to do as quickly as possible when you get started, according to Sandra, is to get bookings with people outside your circle of family and friends. Because they'll have a whole group of people you don't know. Each person who has a party, exposes you to people you don't know. So you are extending your circle of bookings outside of your family. That's when your business is on its way. Because each one of those people is a potential hostess who will introduce you to a group of people you don't know."

When you first get started, what you want to do is to get bookings with people outside your circle of family and friends as quickly as possible.

Two days later, Jenny walked away from the TV and decided to make some phone calls. She phoned each of the ladies who had purchased product from her and asked them openly if they would like to have a party. While most said no, three said they would. They'd had a great time and had been browsing through the catalogue that Jenny had left with them. They wanted another pair of shoes and the hostess offer would get it for them. One booked for the following week, one booked a fortnight out and the other booked for the following month. Jenny immediately booked her hostess calls into her diary.

However, by the end of the month, Jenny got a frantic call from Sarah, echoing a new problem for both of them.

"I can't believe it," Sarah wailed. "I've had three cancellations over the next fortnight! God, it's hard enough to get bookings, let alone lose them at the last minute."

Jenny agreed. "I know. I've just had two cancellations, too. It's gut-wrenching, isn't it. I feel really let down. But you still have to be polite. What were the excuses your hostesses gave?"

"One lady said that she's too busy."

"Well, that's not right. She agreed to the party, she knew what she was doing when she booked it. What's the deal there?" Jenny felt so disappointed for Sarah.

"Another one said that she's got people come to stay and needs to move it."

"Well, at least she didn't cancel. When did she rebook it for?"

"I wasn't able to pin her down to a date. She just said that I should call her back at the end of the month," Sarah said through gritted teeth.

"And the other one has had the roof blown off her house and said it's a bit difficult holding a party with no roof on your house. So I have to call her back in a couple of weeks," Sarah finished.

"Well, that's a legitimate excuse. And at least, she didn't cancel." Jenny asked, "Have you diarised these calls? So you don't forget?"

"Not yet. I'm still reeling from going to have four parties booked over two weeks, down to one!"

Jenny thought for a bit. "Sarah, the ladies who cancelled, at the party where you got their booking, how badly did they want their shoes or the bags they were going to get through being a hostess?"

"One really wanted hers badly. She's the one the roof blew off her house. But the other two," she slowly added as she thought about it, "they were keen but I guess I did rather talk them into it. I felt a bit pushy but at least I got the booking!" Sarah justified to herself.

"That's it then!" Jenny couldn't believe it. "They didn't have a strong Emotional Connection to the products, therefore they had no reason to stick to what they had said!"

"I'm getting sick of hearing about this Emotional Connection." Sarah sounded as frustrated with Jenny as she was with her lost hostesses.

"But don't you see? Those who really connect to the products and really want them, commit to a party. Those who don't really want them, but think they would be nice to have, are only interested in having a party. Therefore, when the slightest obstacle turns up, they drop the party. Those who really want the shoes or bags they have fallen in love with, commit to it and will have the party regardless of what happens. We both know now which one is more likely to cancel."

**Those who really connect to the products, *commit* to a party.
Those who think it would be nice to have, are only *interested*
in having a party.
Which do you think will be the most likely to cancel?**

"The Emotional Connection isn't strong," Jenny finished.

"So, how do we learn to make the Emotional Connection stronger?" asked Sarah. "You can't make them buy."

"No, you can't," agreed Jenny. "But maybe we need to listen more closely to what they say." Jenny felt she had made a breakthrough in understanding, not only how to make more bookings, but on how to prevent them from cancelling.

"One more thing," she added. "Those ladies who cancelled, how thorough were you with your hostess coaching?"

"I didn't quite do it like you do," admitted Sarah. "I just called them the week before, which was when they cancelled. Do you think that's part of the problem?"

"Yes, I do." Jenny sounded excited again. "I think it's part of the success recipe. I wonder what would have happened if you had called them and kept them focused on that pair of shoes they wanted. I wonder if it would have held their motivation."

"Probably. I seem to be doing everything wrong." Sarah sounded miserable. "How do you book parties if you don't have any parties?"

"You have to find new strategies to ask people," gently suggested Jenny. "I had a lady in the dress shop the other day, who commented on my bag. I went back the next day and left her a catalogue and now she's going to have a party. You just have to keep your eyes and ears open for opportunities."

"I don't think I could do that. It's all right for you, you've got much more confidence than I have. I don't think I could do that. I'd feel dreadful," Sarah admitted.

"But I felt uncomfortable doing it the first time, too! But I got a great result. The lady really loved the catalogue and was delighted with her purchase. She ended up buying two! Her friends were really envious. So it was easier the next time." Jenny leaned forward in earnest. "Sarah, you've just got to give it a go. Dig deep and give it a go. You'll not feel good the first time, but it gets easier." Jenny tried not to be too pushy.

"I don't know. I'll see."

"It's how you'll grow the business," urged Jenny. "You need to push against your comfort zones. Don't let how you feel stop you from doing new things."

"Stop! You're starting to sound like one of those new-age gurus," laughed Sarah.

Jenny smiled. "Sorry. I guess I'm just really keen for us both to succeed at this business." And, she thought to herself, if what they say works, then that's what I'll do. Regardless of how I feel about it.

8

Coaching For Bookings

When you first start your party plan business, it is very natural that the first time someone says they want a party, for you to dive in and tell them more about the products, what the hostess rewards are and just get the party booked in. You'll want to get out of there before they change their mind. Flushed with success, we feel that the booking itself is the main thing to focus on. But think back for a moment, who did the most talking? You did. Do you know why she has agreed to have a party? If you are just starting your business, you're probably thinking, who cares! She's booked! That's the main thing. But if you go down this path, you're going to have more than your share of cancellations. And when you start to grow your team, you're not going to be great at training them how to get more bookings, but more importantly, how to keep them.

When someone says they are going to book a party, your first thought should be, why? What is the why behind booking the party? What is her Emotional Connection to? What does she hope to get? Is she carried along with someone else's or your enthusiasm. Or is there a product that she can't afford? Having a party will get this for her. This is the best reason for them to book a party because they have a strong Emotional Connection, which you can reinforce through your hostess coaching.

What is the why behind her booking the party?
What is her Emotional Connection to?

If they have been carried away with the enthusiasm, you'd better meet her for coffee, go over the catalogue together and find something she wants. Or as time passes, If there's nothing special that she wants, she'll focus on all the hassle of having a party instead of focusing on that one special thing she wants. Now, the slightest excuse will cause her to cancel. So it's vital that you find out why she has agreed to have a party, either at the party where she booked, or visit her and take her out for coffee. Take a catalogue with you and find something she wants.

Those who really connect to the product, *commit* to a party. Those who think it would be nice to have, are only *interested* in having a party.

They are not going to have a party because <u>you</u> want them to. They may book it, but they are quite likely to have a change of mind and cancel. The ideal situation is for them to have a party because there is something they want. Remember WIIFM — What's In It For Me? If I have a party, then I will get... Keep this in mind and you'll always be looking to create the Emotional Connection for them. Do that and you'll have far fewer cancellations.

Interest Or Commitment?

Ken Blanchard said, "*There is a difference between interest and commitment. When you're interested in doing something, you do it only when it is convenient. When you're committed to something, you accept no excuses, only results.*"

This is a very important distinction to make in two situations. Firstly, when someone has booked a party, are they interested in having the party? Or are they committed to having the party? This makes a big difference in the type of hostess coaching you do.

Is your hostess interested in having a party? Or is she committed to having a party? This makes a big difference in the type of hostess coaching you will do.

For those who are simply interested, you will have to find an Emotional Connection with them, so they become committed to the party. And the sad fact of the matter is this, some people commit to nothing in their lives. Don't waste time on them. But if you visit them, ask good open-ended questions and really listen to their answers, go through the catalogue with them asking the right questions, you will find something they have an Emotional Connection with.

The other situation to look at through the lens of this distinction, is for your own business. Hopefully, you are fully aware that Jenny is committed to her business, but Sarah is only interested in running hers. Where are you at with your business? Interested or committed?

Where are you at with your business?
Interested or committed?

Now don't be concerned if you realise that while you're enthusiastic about growing a business, you discover that really you are more interested than committed to it. In this day and age, and in the Western world's comfortable lifestyle, and especially as women, we can go through a comfortable life and never commit to anything! Amazing, isn't it. So commitment can seem scary and very new to many of us.

Go back and revisit your goals. Allocate some time to really think about them. What would your life be like if you achieved your goal. Now really think about this. What would you no longer have in your life? Stress and worry? Would you be able to pay the bills on time? Would spending money become painless? With no guilt or negative consequences? Would you have wonderful holidays? A house you loved? A wardrobe filled with designer shoes, bags and clothes?

Really imagine what your life would be like if you achieved your goals. You see, this is an unknown world to you. You've never lived there before. So you have to create a very clear and enticing picture, which increases your desire to make it happen. It doesn't matter if you don't think it's possible. That's another part of the process. Just let your imagination run wild and emotionally put yourself in the picture of the future you would like to have. You have to see it, but more importantly, you have to feel it. You should end up feeling excited, smiling, and a bit scared. That's the right goal.

Next you want to start collecting pictures of your goal. If you have a particular house you want, get pictures of it and either put them in your journal or on a vision board in your office. (I'm calling the spare room your office because I'm assuming that you have set it up as an office by now.)

If you want a particular car, get someone to take a photo of you sitting in that car. Take it for a test drive. See and feel yourself owning that car. Know what colour you want. Know what you are going to wear on your international conference trip that you are going to take your husband on. What cocktails are you going to try? What shopping are you going to do while you are there? Get specific.

That's how to develop commitment. That's how you develop a "no-matter-what-it-takes" attitude. I remember realising at one stage that I was interested rather than committed to a goal, and I listened to a CD by Robert Allan of *The One Minute Millionaire* fame. He said that when you really want to achieve something, imagine that your children's lives depended on it. Wow, that is extreme. But can you feel the intensity that follows from that

65

thought? All of a sudden, you feel very focused, there is no option of not doing the action required to achieve that goal. Now you can see the difference between interest and commitment!

Action

To read more about commitment, read Principle 35 of Jack Canfield's book, *How To Get From Where You Are To Where You Want To Be*. Now if you are already saying that you can't afford to buy another book, there's good news! The library system has his book. You can join the library for free. And you can borrow books, CDs and DVDs for free! So that excuse isn't valid. Sorry.

Getting To Know The Guests

When your hostess holds a party, it is quite likely that you won't know anyone there. As they arrive, they will greet each other as they are quite likely to know everyone there. The ideal party would have you getting to chat to each person and getting to know them a bit. What actually happens at lots of parties I have seen, is that the person selling the products doesn't know how to break into the little chatting groups and holds back. This is missing out on the perfect opportunity to build empathy and start the process of making the Emotional Connection. The first time they really talk to the guests is when they ask them for a sale. Not the ideal. Today, we like to buy from people we know and trust. And that doesn't usually happen right at the end of the sale at the decision-making time. Better to start it earlier.

So, how do you approach a person you don't know and get them chatting? Notice I said, get *them* chatting. Not *you* chatting to them. Not you telling them how *your* week has been or what things have been happening to you lately, or who you are and who your family are and what you do when you are not doing parties!!!! It's not about you, sweetheart! It's all about the guests.

What you want to do is to get to know them, even just a little for two reasons. One is to begin the Emotional Connection to you, so they will trust you and enjoy the party more. Relaxed people buy more! And the second reason is you need to know a bit about them so you know how to sell to them. You know what to talk about when you try to make an Emotional Connection to the products during the party, or when you want to get a party booking from them. And certainly, you want to get them interested in joining the business.

So, here's a useful technique in getting people talking freely and feeling very comfortable talking to you, even though you were a stranger only seconds ago. When we get nervous or uncomfortable, we tend to ask closed questions.

"So, Vinka, do you work?"

"Have you had a good day?"

"Have you heard of our products before?"

"Have you been to a ... party before?"

This will get you a yes or no answer. That's what closed questions do. They require a yes, no or a very short answer. Then they shut the person down. The onus is now back on you to keep the conversation going. But if you are asking closed questions, it's like pulling teeth. Mainly because after a closed question, we get trapped in them and out comes another one. Your lady answers that too and then shuts down. Sound familiar?

Open-ended questions do several things. Firstly, they allow the person to give you a lot of information in a very relaxed manner. That's right, open-ended questions relax the person — and they build empathy. That means that when you ask a good open-ended question, not only do you get a lot of information, the person feels like you are interested in her. Now here's a fact for you. In this day and age of choice, we can buy from whom we want. And most people want to buy from people they like. And if they feel you are interested in them, they will be more willing to buy from you.

Remember me saying that everything you do and say either increases or decreases your sales. Well, if you learn to use open-ended questions well, you will increase your sales, your bookings and especially your recruitment. Because when it comes to talking about them joining the business, the main reason will not be about the products. When someone joins the business, their Emotional Connection will not be with the products. Which is why most people find it difficult to recruit, because they are still in product mode. Just know that you need to know a bit about someone before you can successfully recruit them to your team.

**When someone joins the business,
their Emotional Connection will not be with the products.
Which is why most people find it difficult to recruit,
because they are still in product mode.**

Open-Ended Questions

So, here's a simple but powerful technique to learn. Think of T E D.

T for Tell me about ....

E for Explain ....

D for Describe ....

These are all open-ended questions, which will lead to you getting lots of information without having to ask lots of questions. It becomes a conversation rather than an interrogation. Some examples of questions you could ask are:

"Tell me how you know Nicole (the hostess)."

"Tell me a bit about your job."

"Tell me about your children."

Tell me about ….. is my favourite as it really gets the conversation flowing. You don't have to ask lots, you just ask one question, listen very closely to what they are saying and making a mental note of some of the comments they make. If you don't have a good memory, after a short chat, excuse yourself, make some short notes in a notebook, put it back in your bag then move on to the next person. Always, after a party, sit and make notes on the hostess and as many of her guests as you can remember. I would strongly recommend that you start customer files, listed by hostess. If you keep good information, it will help you get repeat business two, three or four times a year as you will see in a later chapter.

So, just to reiterate, when the guests start arriving, approach one of them, ask an open-ended question. Let them have their say, really listen to what they say. Then excuse yourself and move to the next person. Introduce yourself, ask an open-ended question, (it doesn't matter if you ask the same question of them all), listen carefully, make mental note, etc. You get the idea.

This means that you have truly met most of the guests before the party starts and that makes your presentation even more friendly. They will be more open to your message and you will find your sales will increase. Because you have connected with them, some of them will be interested to hear more about joining the business. That's if you plant the seed and take the opportunity to discover interest.

By now, you may be feeling a bit overwhelmed as it would appear that there are more skills to be learned than you first realised. Don't try to do everything at once. Pick one skill a week that you want to become better at. One skill a week, where you practise it and become better at it, will result in not only business growth, but more importantly, your growth as an effective person.

Don't try to do everything at once.
Pick one skill a week that you want to become better at.

These skills are not just applicable to growing a business, they are applicable to every relationship in your life. So you don't have to practise on customers first. Practise on your family, your friends, on strangers while you are waiting in a queue. And as you practise, watch the effect these questions have on the other person. Watch how they brighten up and respond. Then notice the impact this has on your confidence and self-esteem. This is a truly win/win technique. In a world of busy people where even customers are of little interest in the retail world, to have someone truly interested who makes you feel listened to, is an uplifting experience for most people. Like any new skill, the more you do it, the better you get. It becomes natural. It's just the thing you do when you meet new people. And if you meet someone who is reserved or you feel uncomfortable with, consciously being able to call on open-ended questions will be a godsend.

And the other uses for open-ended questions?

"Susan, tell me why you're going to have a party?" This will tell you what her Emotional Connection is to. Now you'll know what to keep motivating her on in your hostess coaching. But don't rely on your memory, take notes in your customer files. When you do hostess coaching, you should know their Emotional Connection, their kids' names, their husbands' names and their concerns in having the party. And if you ask a series of closed questions to get this information, it will turn into an interrogation, which will destroy empathy rather than build it. Everything you say either increases or decreases your sales.

Another use for open-ended questions? You guessed it, recruiting.

"Susan, tell me why you're interested at looking at the business." This will get her talking. If she's not sure what she wants herself, the long flow of information, which flows from this question, will clarify things for both of you. When you recruit, it is vital that you identify what the Emotional Connection is to, because it will not be the products. The Emotional Connection to the products gets you sales and parties. They do not get you new members to your team. People join the business for a large range of reasons, and if they love the product, that's only the start, That is not the whole reason for joining.

One last use for open-ended questions. Unhappy or complaining customers. You will find that as your business grows, you will get a corresponding increase in unhappy customers or customer complaints. You're dealing with people and you can't keep all the people happy all the time. Even with the best products in the world.

"Susan, I know you're upset. Tell me what has happened." This will allow her to tell her story, or her version of it, and if she gets the chance to pour it out and she feels listened to, that will be satisfying for her. If you interrupt her or disagree with her, you will increase her frustration. So, ask the open-ended question, take notes and let her know you are taking notes (if you're on the phone and she can't see you), and that will make her feel that you are taking her seriously. Get as many facts as you can and tell her you will investigate and call her back. Tell her when you will call her back, and above all, call her when you said you were going to!

By the way, open-ended questions work with kids and partners too. Or if you're single, you'll now realise that the traditional questions of, "Do you come here often?" or "Where do you work?" do not work because you are awkward in asking them but they don't work because they are closed questions, they don't build empathy and they shut people down.

NOTES

NOTES

9

The Roller-Coaster Ride

Jenny was confused. It was weird. Today was so different from
yesterday. She woke and for the first time she was less than enthusiastic
about her party that night. For the first time, she thought wistfully of a night
at home watching TV with Mark and the kids. She'd almost forgotten what
Callum looked like. Her son led a busy life bustling between sport and
friends, so while so many of her evenings were involved being out at parties,
they hadn't spent much time together for quite some time. Mark was being
fabulous and was taking Callum to all his sporting practices and his games.
But Jenny felt like she was missing out on time with him. She just got to
wash his uniform. And today, that wasn't enough.

She tried to shake off her lethargy. She figured maybe she was just
tired. But, to make matters worse, when she got dressed, she couldn't get her
jeans to meet. It was a struggle to zip them up. "No! She couldn't believe it.
"What the..."

How could she have put on weight when she'd been so busy! She
looked sideways at herself in the mirror. She took a good long look at herself.
She really should book in and get her hair trimmed as well. That made her
feel worse. Not only did she not feel good, she didn't look her best either.

As Jenny walked out to the kitchen, she noticed kids' shoes lying in
the lounge, the dirty clothes basket was overflowing, there were dishes all
over the sink and she could see a pile of ironing waiting for her in the family
room. But she had calls to make to her hostesses. And she had a couple of
good leads to follow up on.

"Stuff it!" she put the jug on. "It can wait. I'm not a bloody machine.
I need a break." She'd never been able to ignore the housework. She had
always hated messy houses and couldn't just walk away and hope someone
would see what needed to be done. She had finished the dishes, tidied the
house and was part way through the ironing when Mark, Sinead and Callum
burst through the front door all carrying McDonald's brown bags. Obviously,

while the housework was easily forgotten, their lunch wasn't!

Mark got himself a cold drink from the fridge, yelling over his shoulder at Callum: "Get back here and pick up those joggers!" He turned and saw her watching. "What are you doing?"

"What's it look like?"

He looked around the kitchen. "We were going to do those dishes when we got home. Now I've got to find another job for the kids."

"I didn't know, did I? I just couldn't stand the state of this house." For some reason, tears prickled in her eyes. That just made her more angry. It wasn't fair! Here she was trying to run a business and a household, and they had been out having fun together. And they hadn't brought food any home for her, I'll bet. "Where's my lunch?"

Mark looked surprised. "You don't like McDonald's."

"Well, you could've got me something else."

"I'm not a mind-reader, you know. I didn't even know if you'd be home." He turned and walked out of the room. She heard him call out to Callum: "And get your shoes out of the lounge! Sinead, your turn for the dusting."

Jenny could've kicked herself. She woke up feeling grotty and she had taken it out on Mark. Stuff her business, stuff the ironing. She followed him into the bedroom and curled up against him on the bed. He lay stubbornly with his hands clasped behind his head. No cuddles yet.

"I'm sorry. I guess I'm just feeling sorry for myself. Although I don't know why. The business is going great guns, and you've being so brilliant with the kids. I just feel tired and left out when you all came home like that. And," she fought back tears, "I've put on weight. My jeans are tight!" She couldn't hold back the tears any longer and Mark reached over for her.

"Come here. Time for a cuddle, I think." He gave her a big squeeze. "Now tell me what's wrong."

"I don't know" she sniffed. "It just seems like everything seems wrong since I woke up this morning. I'm sorry. I guess I'm just tired. Maybe it's just too much, taking on this business." As soon as she had said it, Jenny felt worse and the tears fell faster. "But I really wanted to do this well. I don't want to not do it. But maybe I'm just not cut out for it."

"Now, you stop right there."

Mark's stern tone of voice stopped her in her tracks. "You're doing a brilliant job. You've already started bringing in money. You paid for Callum's new joggers and Sinead's schoolbooks. You should be proud of yourself, not feeling sorry for yourself."

Jenny looked at him, surprised. "You know," she sat up and blew her nose. Tucking the tissue back in her pocket, she took stock. "I don't know what's wrong with me. Yesterday I was so focused and excited by what

I'm doing. And I am proud of the fact that I have started contributing to the finances of our family." She gave Mark a shaky smile and sniffed. He grinned.

"But it's as if I woke up on a different planet this morning. All I could see was the negatives. What's not been done. It's like I could only focus on what was wrong, not what was right. And do you know what was worse?" she asked Mark, who was wise enough not to even try to guess. "I didn't care about any goals, any aspirations I had about the business. If someone had mentioned goals to me, I would have thrown something at them. I just felt bad and that was everything."

"How about we go out and celebrate and add a bit of excitement to your life. Why don't you come with us to Callum's water polo game this afternoon and I'll buy you an ice-cream. Or does your tight jeans mean you're not allowed any treats for a while?"

Jenny gave him a big hug. He was trying to be so tactful. A chocolate dip ice-cream was exactly what she needed. She'd go for a good fast walk in the morning. But, she also needed to get back and start some sessions at the gym. She had stopped going once her business started getting busy. In fact, she hadn't been and had her hair done, and a manicure was out of the question as far as time went. Her life was a bit out of balance. She'd got too busy. Time for a review, she thought.

And although on the surface, she was brighter, she still didn't feel good about herself. The afternoon at the water polo match was a good break and it felt great to be together on a family outing. It felt even better to be able to yell and support Callum at the same time. To scream threats at the boy guarding him, pushing him underwater to get at the ball. She was on her feet in an instant, yelling at the referee: "That was a foul! Are you watching the game for goodness sake?" she screamed. Mark tugged at her shorts until she sat down with a thump. "Well, for goodness sake. He wasn't even looking!"

Mark just looked at her, his eyebrows raised. She grinned. "This is great, just what I needed." She turned back to the game. "Come on, boys! We need another goal!" on her feet yelling again.

That night, while she felt better than she had this morning, her energy was definitely less than usual. But she checked her box before putting it in the car, and revisited her goals for the party before she left. She had a bit of difficulty finding the place, and it had got dark before she got there. Unfortunately, the hostess hadn't done what she was asked to do, tie a bunch of balloons to her letterbox so those who hadn't been there before, could find it easily even in the dark. So she was a bit later than she liked to be. But once inside and setting up her display, Jenny found herself drawn into the mindset of getting to know these women better.

This was a new group for her and she knew none of them. But by the end of the evening, she felt she had a new circle of friends. It had been a smaller party but she did get another booking. It was still another step forward, she reminded herself as she drove home. Every sale moved her closer to her goals. Every booking, pushed her forward to her goals. No party was wasted. You either learned something from it, or at the very least, it was good practise. And if you got some sales and a booking, that was a good party.

The next morning, Jenny sent in her orders and marked her hostess coaching reminders in her diary. She made a quick phone call to thank the hostess for having the party and had a short chat. She went through the party box and replaced the catalogues, order forms and everything they had used at the party. She made a few hostess calls, tidied her office then sat down and opened her journal. She reread her vision of what her life would be like when she achieved her goals. She spent some time imagining living that life. She experienced the thrill of travelling to international conference. She loved the feel of writing out cheques for the bills two days before they were due. She loved the idea of going shopping with Sinead and Callum for their sports gear, with no reluctance or budgetary restrictions. And most of all, she loved the feeling of walking into her future wardrobe and seeing it filled with designer clothes with shoes lined up beneath and, sitting next to them, the gorgeous matching bags. Her teal sports car was parked in the garage and she was planning their next family holiday. And finance was not an issue.

Jenny sighed, a soft smile on her face. That's why she was doing it. She flicked through her figures and couldn't believe how well she was doing. She counted the months since she started and reminded herself that she had not known anything about either selling or how shoes and bags were produced only a few months before. And now she was on track, right on track. It felt good. She felt more complete that she had ever before. She didn't analyse it too much, she just wanted to enjoy it. And to think that yesterday she could've walked away and given it all up. How strange, she thought. To go from one mindset to such an extreme in such a short time, and back again. She'd started her period this morning, so that probably had a lot to do with it. But she hadn't noticed any change the month before. Maybe she had been driving herself a bit too hard. Maybe part of her planning should revolve around her getting some quality time looking after herself.

Jenny resolved to get back into her gym routine but first she booked herself into the hairdresser. Actually, she thought, brightening up, that would be a great place to leave a catalogue. Yes, she was definitely back on track.

Which was just as well as Sarah phoned and suggested they get together for a coffee. Jenny certainly didn't want to be in a brown patch when meeting Sarah. She knew enough now about their relationship to know that she needed to have good armour against Sarah's lack of motivation. Jenny could now clearly see her complacency and was prepared to handle any whinging that might arise. Jenny now looked at their relationship quite differently. She was looking forward to seeing Sarah and was hoping that all was going well. But she wasn't going to let Sarah impact on her in any way. As it was, she discovered that Sarah was struggling with some new issues.

Sarah explained that after their last session, she was brimming full of confidence and dived back into the business. She showed her husband the sales that some reps were making and booked several parties from some of the leads she had. However, she was losing her confidence again.

"I just feel like I don't know enough about the shoes and how they are made," she explained to Jenny. "I keep forgetting what they are called and I don't know the catalogue well enough. People have been asking me questions I can't answer and I feel like I should stop doing parties until I know more. The company should give us more information," she complained.

"But what about your manual?" asked Jenny. "There's stacks of information in there. So much, in fact, I haven't even read it all yet," she admitted.

"But I had one lady who wanted to know so much detail. She wanted to know about the type of leather which is used, about where they are made!" She threw up her hands, "I don't know these things. I don't have enough product knowledge and I want to know what J'Adore is going to do about it."

"Have you spoken to Sandra?"

"No, not yet. But they should have more information." Sarah screwed up the serviette so obviously frustrated.

"But Sarah, she's the first person you should be speaking to," answered Jenny. "Whenever you have a problem, you must go to your upline. I know we are starting our own businesses, but in party plan, you're not on your own. You're part of a team. That's the beauty of the business. That's why we can start a business in something we don't know much about at the start. That is the very reason that you need to make an effort to get along to training. I learned so much product knowledge at the last meeting. I suspect that you learn more at each meeting. And you meet the women whose businesses are flying. Some of them are doing unbelievably well. I sat and picked the brains of one older lady and I got heaps of great ideas. Ideas on how to get more bookings for parties to name just one." Jenny shook her head. "Don't worry if you don't know it all. It'll come as you get more experienced."

"Yeah, well it's all right for you..."

"Don't you dare say that again." Jenny looked fierce and Sarah sat back and blinked. This wasn't the Jenny she knew. "You say that every time you don't want to face your lack of confidence. It's not all right for me! I studied the script and learned it by heart. I have analysed every party I have done and every one I've watched and have practised different techniques until I saw what worked. It's not all right for me. You make me sound as if it has all been a breeze for me. It hasn't, I have worked at it!" Jenny sat back and took a deep breath. She waited to see what Sarah would do. "When you say that, you negate all the work I have put in, and I resent that. I've worked hard," she said again.

'I... I'm sorry." Sarah looked stunned. "I've never thought about it that way before."

Jenny leaned forward, trying to get her point across. "Sarah, I've been every bit as nervous as you have been. I've lost my confidence and been overwhelmed so many times, feeling like I don't know what I'm really doing. But, I just go back to my goals, I relearn the script, I talk to Sandra and I refocus. I figure that I'll fake it until I make it. I mean, anything major that I don't know, I go straight to Sandra or one of the other reps that I have met at training and I keep asking until I get an answer. But the point is that you have to keep going despite the fact that you feel like you don't know enough. That's called growth!"

You have to keep going despite the fact
that you feel like you don't know enough.
That's called growth!

They were both looking at each other when the chair at their table was pulled back and Mark sat down. He looked from one to the other, stood back up and said: "I'll just get myself a coffee. You both look like you need another one."

Sarah grimaced. "Sorry Jenny. I didn't mean to make it seem like you haven't worked at it. I know you have, I really admire your focus and determination. But I just feel so alone at times. I really struggle with it and it just makes me feel..." She broke off as tears threatened. Jenny reached across and squeezed her hand.

"Don't worry about it. I was sobbing into Mark's shoulder last week, too. No one said it was going to be easy. For goodness sake, we're starting a new business. That's no small thing. Of course we are going to go through a bit of a roller-coaster of emotions."

Mark returned with three coffees and sat down again. He looked warily at the two women. "Is everything okay?" he asked cautiously.

"Yes, we're just saying how hard it seems at time, feeling like we don't know what we're doing," Jenny said, watching Sarah take a deep breath and pull herself together again.

"But haven't you got someone coaching you?" Mark inquired.

"I discouraged her actually," said Sarah. "I didn't want anyone breathing down my neck. How could I have been so stupid?" She looked at Jenny.

"Well, I must admit that I haven't taken full advantage of the support either. I guess I just wanted to prove I could do it on my own."

"Women! Honestly, you both complain that you don't know what you're doing but you're not using the services of the person who can teach you. And another thing," he added as the women grinned sheepishly at each other. "I think you get too excited about your income and the conference. Then when it becomes harder than you think, you die off. You need to be taking a more measured, logical approach rather than just riding on the passion."

"Anything else you think we should be aware of?" asked Sarah. Jenny watched fascinated as Sarah really seemed to be listening to Mark.

"Think past the goodies. Start thinking much further down the track, past when you get the goodies you're aiming for. You've got to ask yourself whether you're prepared to put in the work, which will get you the goodies. You need at least a thee-year plan because once you clear the fence, all of a sudden, it will become easier and the money will come rolling in. And the bookings and the recruitment too," he added.

"Don't get me wrong, I'm not saying that you shouldn't be passionate, but I'm saying that you have to take a practical approach and be prepared to put in the hard yards. I see so many people start something up and as soon as they discover that they have to work hard to get it up and running, they aren't prepared to do the hard work which will get them their goals." He took a sip of coffee and looked at the two surprised women.

"Well you did ask."

10

Coaching For The Ups And Downs

When you start your business, you need to be prepared for all the things which will impact you emotionally. Things like hormones, family needs, pressure of so many demands on your time, depression and the guilt of not being able to be all things to all people. In other words, some days you'll be focused and energised. Other days will be plain bad hair days. Your clothes won't fit, you can't find a car park, too many bills in the mail and who gives a damn about goals anyway.

It is important to understand that how women handle their problems, can be quite different as compared to how men do. When a man has a problem, he narrows his focus until he is totally focused on just that problem. However, when a women has a problem, she widens her focus. She looks around and doesn't just see that problem, she takes on board ALL the problems she has. Or perceives she has at that moment in time. She widens her focus to include all her problems. This is stressful so her next step is to find someone to talk to. She wants to tell someone about these problems because this lowers her stress levels. Then she can get to and start solving them.

As a woman in business, I have a rule which I have found has been invaluable for me. I will not make any business decisions unless I'm feeling on top of it all. In other words, if I'm not feeling good, and I find myself worrying about a range of business issues, I just get my head down and get through the work until I come out the other side. I now stop myself making some knee-jerk reaction based on poor, emotional decision-making.

When you're not feeling at your best, your decision-making won't be in top form either because you can only see and feel the negatives. This is not a time to make any decisions. This is the time to just do what you have to do and leave decisions for another day.

At the start of this book, I said that business is a great teacher. But many people simply miss the lessons. They go into business with one party plan company, do well but for a range of reasons, become unhappy with the company and leave. Only to join another party plan company and do really well until they become unhappy with the company and leave. Hello! A pattern. What is happening here is that the business is offering them a challenge and their response is to walk away. Now, that's not what they tell themselves. We all believe our own excuses, absolutely. We truly believe the lies we tell ourselves. But look at the pattern. Here is a talented person with great potential for success. But they are allowing themselves to be stopped by something they decide is unacceptable.

As strange as it may sound, if they stayed, they would become very successful. They were already doing well when they react emotionally to some issue they aren't happy with. So they are already doing well. The problem is not that they're not earning good money as often they are sensationally successful very quickly. But maintaining that success brings them face to face with something they don't want to face. So they walk. If you have this pattern in your life, I highly recommend that you participate in some one-on-one coaching. Break through the pattern and allow yourself to become as successful as your ability indicates you can become.

**Maintaining that success brings them face to face
with something they don't want to face. So they walk.**

The fact of the matter is that you will have good days and you will have bad days. What is important is what you do on your bad days. Firstly, don't make any ad hoc decisions about your business. Simply, look at your list of things to do, and at least do some of them. Then move on to doing something that you enjoy doing. You might want to catch up with your housework. All right, I know I said do something you enjoy, but catching up with some things you have got behind on, will make you feel better. And that should be your goal at times like this. Do things that make you feel better — long-term. Not a short burst of pleasure like binging on chocolate or hammering the credit card. That will be a short burst of pleasure followed by a long burst or regret and consequences. Go and have coffee with a friend. Go to an art gallery or somewhere that feeds your soul. For me it is either an inspirational bookshop, a library or a beach. Just stop your mind and experience. Spend time with someone who makes you laugh. Go to the movies, on your own if no-one is available. Go for a walk, have a spa, go to the gym if that's your thing.

Self-Sabotage

Which brings me to self-sabotage. Why would someone who says she wants to be successful, and is showing all the signs of being successful, walk away to another company, only to move on yet again when she starts to be successful again. Most people think that fear of failure is the big one, but in this day and age, with the opportunities we can now choose from, I believe that fear of success is much more threatening for many women. What if you were much more talented than you had ever believed? What if you were much more skilled than you had believed possible? What if you were able to attract huge success into your life? For many people, this is a very frightening thought for many reasons. Some would say that this isn't a frightening thought, but then turn around and do the exact opposite of what is needed to be successful. Party plan is a great arena to meet people who convincingly tell you what they do or don't do, and then proceed to do the exact opposite. It is amazing, but we believe our own lies to ourselves, completely.

Why is this? Because in the party plan industry, you choose what you are going to do. You choose at what level you want to work at, at what level of success you feel comfortable with. And while there is not a boss to blame for anything, many times you hear them blame the company, the product, their upline – anyone or anything rather than examining their own conflicting behaviour. Having to face it would mean doing something about it. Which would mean that they would end up more effortlessly successful which is what they are trying to avoid in the first place.

Let's look at the most common self-sabotage behaviours.

Poor Time Management

This is the most acceptable excuse in today's market because we all know that we lead busy lives, so on the surface it would seem that this is a genuine reason for not doing something. However, this just says that you have put what you didn't want to do at a very low priority. If it was a high priority, you would have made time to do it. Let me give you an example. You've got a busy week coming up. You've already got lots to do, the kids have sports events, birthday parties, just for starters. And your husband comes home and tells you that the boss has invited you both out for dinner. There is a promotion coming up and it looks like your husband might be promoted! This is something he's been hoping for, for some time. And you haven't anything appropriate to wear to an expensive restaurant, which is less than five years old.

Do you think you will find time in your busy timetable to get out and buy a new outfit? Absolutely, without question. Because it has just become a high priority. You don't want to look dowdy in front of the boss and his wife. And you want to feel confident in yourself.

But if there's something we don't want to do, such as hostess coaching or following up leads, we say we couldn't do it because we were too busy. Too busy is just an excuse. What you are really saying is that you never made it a high enough priority. And if you can admit that, then you can examine what you are doing and why. Are you just playing at being in business? Are you filling in time?

Too busy is just an excuse.

Not Planning Or Setting Goals

If you've joined a good party plan company, your upline will have talked to you about setting goals and creating a plan for your month. When someone has been successful at something and they give you advice, does it make sense to ignore this advice? No. But you'll have reasons, justifications and excuses, which will make complete sense to you, and you'll believe these self-lies absolutely. What goal-setting and planning will do, is to begin to create some vision and develop self-discipline. Just doing the actual exercise of setting goals takes self-discipline. And regardless of the results, developing self-discipline is an important part of running a new business. Because there are going to be many things you are not going to like doing. And if you don't have the self-discipline to get through them, your business is certainly going to fail. When you first try something you've not done before, it can often seem like hard work. It's a nuisance and you can't see how it really makes a difference. What difference does it make if you set goals? What difference does it make if you write them down? What difference does it make if you write in a journal? Well, the successful people, tell us it makes all the difference in the world. So, if they say it's important, you need self-discipline to get started. But once you've got into the habit of doing this exercise, it suddenly is not hard work any more. It just becomes the way you work. And you keep doing it because you have now proven to yourself that this is a very successful action. Without acting on this advice and without the planning and goal-setting, you will not develop the self-discipline needed to create a successful business.

This means that you are riding on passion and not taking a practical and logical approach to your business. You are not laying a good foundation to build your business on. Because in party plan, YOU are the foundation of the business. So your growth and your development are vital to the growth of the business. Otherwise, you will be just all the other wannabes, a comet hurtling across the sky only to burn out before getting all the way across. A breathtaking ride that you can talk about to your friends for years to come, but a waste of talent, energy and everyone's time. And because you haven't emerged from your comfort zone or learned any new skills, you remain stuck in the place you don't want to be. Continuing to lead an unfulfilling life of quiet desperation. Don't go there. For the sake of developing some self-discipline, it's so worth it.

Not Attending Training Sessions

Do you attend as many training sessions as possible? Or is your attendance erratic to say the least. First, let's get past the excuses. If I tell you that training sessions will help you become more successful in this business, stop and look at the excuses you have for missing the last training session you didn't attend. Again, family is a very acceptable excuse. As women, we let you off the hook because we know the demands that family put on our time. So when we say, I've got Callum's activity to prepare for, most women will be understanding. But didn't you really end up watching TV?

When you get to training, look around the room. How many people are in that room? 20, 50, 150? Well, guess what? They all have families. And some of them don't have a partner to support them in looking after their kids. And they still got to training. In fact, it's often the case that those with the most excuses (if they wanted to use them) are those who are most consistent with their attendance at training. They seriously want to become successful. They don't make excuses, they make an appearance. Tired, overworked and with every excuse under the sun, they want to learn and succeed.

They don't make excuses, they make an appearance.

Leader Or Manager?

In business you hear lots of discussions about the difference between whether you are a strong Manager or a strong Leader. But you don't hear about it in party plan and I believe that this is a vital concept to know about so you can work on your weaker side, which will result in the faster growth of your business. We all lean to one of these two concepts, Manager or Leader. A natural Leader has the ability to inspire people, to motivate them to want to get into the business and achieve their goals. They are able to pass their enthusiasm on to others and leave others on a high after being with them. When you have been around a natural Leader, they leave you feeling refocused and re-energised. But if you simply run on passion, you will not do all the basics, the boring things you need to do to support a successful business. In other words, if you are a natural Leader, you need to develop the skill of being a good Manager. A good Manager develops systems and takes a logical approach to running the business. Taking care of details.

A Manager	A Leader
Tells or instructs	Coaches
Has an operational focus	Has an inspirational focus
Aims for efficiency	Aims for guidance
Doing things right	Doing the right things
Compliance	Thinking outside the square
Manages the workflow	Manages the people
Focuses on the HOW	Focuses on the WHY
Wants to fix things	Wants to understand

Stop and think about some of the successful people you see in party plan. Some people are naturally inspirational but their teams may not be able to copy them. They will be different and may feel they need more detailed guidance than they get.

Then you have the natural Managers. They give you the systems and what to do step-by-step to make the business grow. But some of their team may also be looking for more inspiration and energy from them. They want more innovative ideas on how to get leads and grow their business.

To grow your team successfully, you need to tailor your training sessions for both kinds of people. You need some systems and step-by-step instructions, which some will find boring, and you need enthusiasm, fun and innovative ideas. To be successful, you need to develop the flexibility to have a mix of both. All the time. In your training, in your coaching, in your presentations, in your recruiting.

So it is important to identify which of your natural strengths lean towards for many reasons. Firstly, it will help you understand if you are not getting what you want from your upline. The reason may be that your upline is your opposite. If you are a natural Leader brimming with enthusiasm and energy, you're not going to enjoy training sessions that cover systems, scripts and step-by-step training. You are looking for enthusiasm, passion and action! In fact, a natural Manager is exactly what you need to balance your strengths. But if you're not aware of this, you'll just feel dissatisfied with your upline and possibly go on to negatively judge the company as well. How you feel is not a good indicator of how you are doing. With any luck, if you are a natural Leader, you'll have a partner who is your opposite. That's why women who are successful at party plan, very often are those who are fully supported by their partners. And their partners may very well be filling their opposite and filling the gap of what their style is.

How you feel is not a good indicator of how you are doing. Too often, we judge how we are doing, by how we feel.

We so often judge how we are doing by how we feel. And if you are not feeling good about working with your upline, you need to understand that if you are opposites, then you will not be getting what you need from her. You need to walk her through what you need from her. Do not be worried about upsetting her. Believe me, she wants you to be successful because that will make her and her team more successful. But she needs to know what you need from her, and how you need her to be as an effective upline.

If, however, you are a natural Manager, you may have an upline who is a natural Leader. But you won't be looking for inspiration. You want the systems and the step-by-step processes. You will want to know how to keep track of your sales and what is the best way of setting up your office. Again, it is vital for you to guide your upline to give you what you need from her.

Secondly, you need this knowledge to help you grow your business. If you don't understand your strengths and weaknesses, you won't know what to work on to improve your results. There are not good or bad ways of doing things, only consequences. If you don't like the consequences or the results you are getting, you need to face and address your weaknesses, which will be getting in the road of your success.

NOTES

NOTES

NOTES

11

Building Your Own Team

During the next few weeks, Sarah and Jenny met regularly at Jenny's place to assess what they needed to do to keep their businesses growing. While the parties were usually successful in sales, Sarah was still having problems getting bookings and, as yet, had no inquiries from anyone about joining the business. It was an enjoyable partnership and Jenny enjoyed sharing the knowledge and information with Sarah. Although, she frequently got frustrated with Sarah, who avoided doing some of the things she should have done.

Jenny wondered if she was getting a bit critical or too judgmental. After all, she wasn't perfect either. But, her brain replied, at least you do make yourself do some of the things you don't want to, and often. That extra activity was what she believed is what leads to more business.

Today, Jenny was so excited as she was having coffee with the lady who had inquired about joining the business. "This might be the start of my team," Jenny said, her eyes shining. "I'm going to have the best training. I want people to develop their self-confidence so much more quickly. I'm sure that would be much less stressful for them. What do you think?"

Sarah looked at her, "What do I think? I think I haven't even had a nibble of interest about someone joining the business."

"Okay," challenged Jenny. "How many people did you ask at your last party?"

"What?" Sarah looked taken aback.

"Well, you're just complaining that you've had no interest. How much interest have you been drumming up? How many people did you ask at your last party? What do you say about joining the business in your presentation?" Her questions came in rapid succession.

"I told you," said Sarah. "I don't feel comfortable following their script. I tell them a bit about why I joined but then I talk about the products and the hostess offers. Isn't that enough? Can't people see what a great business it is, for themselves?"

"What you're really saying, is can't they do your job for you?" Jenny said softly.

"And who turned you into the recruiting police?" Sarah sounded annoyed.

"Sarah, you were complaining and all I did was to point out to you that maybe the reason you are not getting inquiries is because you are not doing the things that generate inquiries."

Sarah responded quickly: "And all this from someone who has had a grand inquiry rate of one!"

"Yep, only one at this stage. But at least I know exactly what I did that generated that inquiry. If you don't do the work, you can't complain about the results." Jenny knew she was pushing it but she so wanted Sarah to take responsibility and be honest with herself. Complaining was like taking a pill — you feel better but nothing has changed. She did not want to support Sarah in letting herself off the hook. Even if it meant losing the friendship. That's not where I'm at anymore, Jenny reminded herself.

"Maybe," Sarah admitted. "Perhaps it's is time for me to go back and give it a try."

Jenny knew that she couldn't count on Sarah actually going back and learning the script but she hoped that she would do exactly that. But when Sarah didn't show up for training that week, Jenny couldn't help feeling disappointed. Sarah was letting herself down. Couldn't she see that. She dragged her mind back to what the speaker was saying.

"How many people here think we offer great hostess gifts?"

Every person in the room put their hands up. "How many of you first held a party because of the hostess gifts?" Jenny glanced around the room and saw that most people had their hands up. "How many of you have someone interested in having a party but can't quite get them across the line?" Again, everybody put their hands up. "Would you like a tip which will increase your bookings for parties?" A great shout came from the group, "YES!"

"Okay, let's walk through the process of booking a party. Imagine you are sitting at a party and you are interested in having a party yourself. Only interested, mind you. You're not convinced yet. You are told about the hostess rewards you're going to get and this is the main reason you are interested. You have a pair of shoes you want to get. And you know if you have a party, at the very least, you'll get them for half price. And you really want those shoes. Now let me ask you this. How many people in the room have teenage sons?" About half the people put up their hands.

"How do you think they would respond, if you asked them to wash your car and you'll give them a reward next week?" There was laughter and murmuring around the room. "I'd still have a dirty car!" one woman called out. Laughter echoed around the room as most nodded their agreement.

"So isn't that a bit the same? Hold a party and I'll give you a reward a couple of weeks after the party when it's time for delivery of your shoes?" The room had gone still as this sunk in. But what was she suggesting, wondered Jenny.

She reached down and pulled a bag out from behind the podium. But it wasn't just any bag, it was gorgeous. "My show bags have increased my bookings without question." She held two bags up. They were brightly coloured metallic carry bags. One was shiny and purple and the other was gold. She lifted a bright metallic jade green one with chord handles and they had tissue paper bursting from them. They looked sumptuous, glamorous and really tempting. Not only did Jenny find herself wondering what was in them, she wanted one.

"Now let me tell you what is in them," the speaker continued. "This is basically a hostess training kit. I have catalogues for her to share with people who can't come to the party. I have the hostess brochure, and I have the recruitment information. I know that what goes into this bag, gets read. So I put in all the literature I want them to read. There are order forms so she can take orders from people who can't attend and I put a hostess instruction sheet in there — Tips on How to Run a Successful Party. I also put in some chocolates, bubble bath sachets, plus any other goodies I might have picked up cheaply. Depending on the hostess, I might also put in a little gift, which would be meaningful to her. The whole bag probably costs me $5-10."

"But imagine being at a party. In my presentation, I hold up my show bags and I say: "Three lucky ladies will leave tonight carrying these fabulous show bags. But you will only get them if you book your own party tonight and it is booked for within the next fortnight."

Jenny was spellbound. She couldn't believe what a great idea it was. The speaker continued: "I have ladies rush at me after my presentation and they've picked out which colour show bag they want. Depending on the size of the party, I have two or three on the table at the back of the display, but they are so successful, that I always have two or three more in the boot of the car. I've even had a couple of ladies arguing over a show bag. So I always put out fewer rather than more because then it seems like they are more excusive. There's not enough to go around. And they walk out the door, swinging their bags, pleased as punch." She waited a moment and the crowd was totally silent absorbing this new information. "How often do you get given a gorgeous gift like this? When you have a baby? When you have a 50th wedding anniversary? Why shouldn't we get gifts that look this fabulous more often? We deserve it. So, what woman wouldn't want to walk out the door with one of these show bags? How special do you think it makes you feel?"

Jenny was astounded. What a great tip. Why hadn't someone told her that before? Every time she came to training, she learned one more thing about improving her business. She couldn't wait to make up her own show bags. It just made sense when you thought about it.

After the training was over, Jenny saw Sandra and walked over to her through the ladies lining up for a coffee and biscuit.

"Hi Jenny," Sandra had a great grin on her face. "How's our champion sales lady?" She was referring to Jenny's last party. She had broken her own record and got $1,500 of sales. Plus she got the recruitment inquiry.

"Sandra, I'm going great. But tonight's been a bit of an eye-opener. I'm sure that there are many experienced ladies here who could give me lots of tips. I love the idea of the show bag. It just makes so much sense."

Sandra shook her head. "You know Jenny, there are any number of ladies in this room who could give you all sorts of tips. But most new people simply don't take the time to ask."

"Sandra, who in this room is really good at recruiting? I want to talk to someone who's breaking records and see what they're doing. You know I have just got my first interview, but I want to grow a team and I want to learn from someone who's doing it really well."

"Come with me." She walked her across the room and approached a large lady who was chatting to the person next to her. "Helen, this is Jenny. She wants to pick the brains of a good recruiter. Jenny, this is Helen. Helen recruited nine people this month, seven last month. I think she's the lady you want to talk to." Sandra pulled out a chair next to Helen for Jenny and moved on.

"Nine people? You recruited nine people this month? And seven people the month before?" Jenny was astounded. She'd expected some sort of glamorous creature who would be the kind of role model she was looking for. Helen was a large lady which if she was honest, she would've passed in the street without a second glance. While she looked friendly and honest, Jenny realised she had some complete misconceptions of what it took to be a success. "How do you do that? I'd love to have some tips if you have time."

Helen turned to her, smiling a little. "It's not a big secret," she said. "She leaned towards Jenny, and Jenny leaned forward to the secret she was obviously going to hear. "You just ask."

"Pardon?"

"You just ask. You set everything up so they are exposed to the idea of the business. You plant seeds in your presentation. You have a notice on the table that says: "Want to earn some extra money to party and wear fabulous shoes and bags?" You have a clipboard that they can lean on to write their order, which lays out all the benefits of joining the business. You ask every person who places an order, and especially those who don't place an order because they can't afford it. You ask. You ask. You ask your hairdresser, the waitress who brings your coffee, your friends who say they're broke. You just keep asking."

"It's really that simple?" Jenny frowned. "I've got my first interview with a lady tomorrow and yet it seems to me that I have been asking."

Helen looked at her. How Jenny answered her next question would indicate how much time she would spend coaching her. "Think back for a moment to that last party where you got your inquiry. How many women did you ask to join the business?"

Jenny thought back. "There was the lady I'm meeting. Another one who said she couldn't afford the bag she wanted, so I suggested she look at the business. And one other whom I thought might be interested. In fact, I'm still not convinced she isn't interested. She's going to have a party next week, so I'm going to talk to her again."

"And how many people were there at the party?"

"Eight plus the hostess."

"So you ignored five potential team members. You asked three, you got one solid inquiry and have another possibility from that three. Not bad," summarised Helen, watching Jenny closely.

Jenny was shocked. She'd thought she'd done well by asking three people.

"If I'd been getting those statistics when I'd first started, I'd have double the team I've got by now. Like most people, I'd try to guess which people to ask. I'd make assumptions about the guests, which ones might be good potential, and which ones weren't. If there's one thing I've learnt the last year or two, those who join the business don't come with a tag, which says: "Ask me!" It's often the most unlikely ones who join and do well. The ones you know could cream it, aren't interested for a range of reasons. Don't make judgments on who to ask, and who you avoid asking. Ask them all. Now go and do some more parties, and come and tell me at the next training session how many people you've recruited."

Jenny felt a mixture of emotions. She found it hard to believe it was that simple. But she couldn't deny that Helen's summary was correct. She did pick and choose whom she was going to ask. She did make assumptions on who was going to buy and who wasn't. And she had been quite wrong several times. On the other hand, she was excited and grateful that Helen had taken the time to give her some coaching. Even if she was a bit abrupt.

"Thanks Helen. I'll see you in a month." But Helen had already turned away and was in deep conversation with the person next to her. Jenny felt dismissed. But she was resolved to try what Helen had told her. At her next party, she would ask every person to consider joining the business. In fact,

Jenny was startled to think that she hadn't thought of this earlier. She was going to go back and make contact with every hostess she'd had and ask them to consider joining the business. Of course, they were the logical people to start with! And after that, she was going to phone every customer she'd had so far that she hadn't asked, which was most of them, she thought a bit sheepishly, and she was going to ask every one to consider joining her team. Jenny made a target there and then to recruit at least four more people within the next month.

The next day, Jenny met Nicole for coffee to discuss the business. She remembered she needed to focus on Nicole first rather than rattling on about the business and talking too much. She didn't want to seem pushy and try to "sell" her on joining, she wanted Nicole to <u>want</u> to join her team. She knew that Nicole's youngest was starting school in a couple of months and she had been considering getting a part-time job. The perfect candidate!

When Jenny turned up for coffee, she made sure she was wearing her favourite shoes and bag set as they always received comments. When they were settled with their coffees, they just chatted for a moment, then Jenny took the plunge and started her process. "So Nicole, how do you feel about Jonathon starting school? Excited or apprehensive?"

Nicole laughed. "Both! I don't want my baby to grow up too fast, and I want them to take good care of him. But, it does mean it's another step towards getting my life back."

"What are you going to do?" Jenny could see that Nicole was a bit nervous about what she faced.

"I don't know. I've started to go through the Sits Vacant but I just can't see myself in an office job. And I only want part-time. I don't want Jonathon and Kim coming home to an empty house. They come first regardless of what I do." She hesitated. "But I've got to start earning a bit of money. Interest rates have risen and our mortgage is sucking us dry. We used to have small luxuries, but even those are disappearing now."

"I know you loved our shoes. Have you considered party plan?"

"No, I've only heard of make-up and Tupperware and neither of those really appeal to me. I mean I know they are both really good products because I have been to parties. I've got Tupperware in my cupboards and I wear Nutrimetics. But I just can't see myself doing those kind of parties."

Jenny bit the bullet and asked: "Could you see yourself wearing our shoes and doing our parties?"

"Now that sounds good to me. I'd love that but I don't know anything about shoes or bags. Except how to wear them," she chuckled.

Jenny started to reassure her. "Neither did I when I first started. But the company provides all the information and the training and now I feel very confident talking about it. And I'm on my way to earning an extra $1,400 this month over and above what I had set as a target. What would you do with an extra $1,400 a month?" Jenny leaned forward and added: "That you have earned at a time which suited you, allowing you to be home for Jonathon and Kim."

Nicole looked at Jenny for a moment. "That sounds too good to be true," she said slowly.

Jenny sat back and smiled. "I'm glad you said that. It doesn't just happen. You have to book parties and make it happen. You do have to work at it, but I must admit, most of the time it doesn't feel like work. You've seen the parties, they're great. Love doing them. But there is more you have to do behind the scenes to make the business happen. But, you know, I'm looking for people to join my team who want to have more fun while they earn. Who want to learn new skills and have the self-discipline to learn how to run their business successfully. And who want to mix with other successful women. I'll support and train you, and the company... well, let me tell you what the company offers. Apart from the shoes and bags, it's one of the reasons I joined."

Jenny got out her brochures and walked Nicole through the benefits of joining. She showed her the compensation plan, the annual conference and the international conference. As she showed Nicole all the benefits, she made a note of what tweaked her interest the most. And it seemed that Nicole needed to make some extra money and still be home for Jonathon and Kim.

"Well, what do you think? Would you like to be part of my team with your own business?" Jenny asked.

Nicole smiled nervously. "I'd love to. It sounds just what I'm looking for, but are you sure I can do this?"

Jenny reassured her again and they filled out the Representative Application Form together. "Nicole, I'm going to call you tomorrow, and if you have any doubts, or any questions, I'm there for you. Just remember, I really want you to be successful at this. I want to see you soar past $1,400 a month. I want to see you earning $2,500 by your third month. How does that sound?"

"Wonderful!" Nicole beamed.

"We'll do it together. Take these brochures home and show them to Morris. If he's got any questions also, I can come around and we can all discuss it until he's happy too."

Nicole replied: "I think he'd be fine. He's been as torn as I have over me going back to work. We both know that we need the money but we don't want the kids coming home to an empty house. He suggested a home-based business but we've not really known what we should do. I think he'll be pleased with this idea."

Jenny turned on her mobile again and ordered another coffee after

Nicole had left. She'd done it! She had her first team member. How exciting. She was going to share all her knowledge and systems with Nicole. And she was going to find more new team players. Just then her mobile rang. It was a message from Sarah.

"Hi, Jenny, it's Sarah. I thought I should phone and tell you that I'm dropping out of the whole party plan scene. It's not really working out for me. No lectures please! I know it's good for you but it's just not right for me. Speak to you later."

Jenny sipped her coffee. She was disappointed about Sarah but not surprised. "It doesn't work out if you don't do the work, Sarah," she muttered to herself. She felt Sarah had squandered a great opportunity. However, she had started her new team now and they deserved all her attention and energy. Her business was now going to grow in leaps and bounds. She smiled to herself. It was time to set new income goals.

12

Coaching For Recruiting

If you're not getting inquiries to join the business, perhaps you're not doing the things which generate inquiries. If you don't do the work, you can't complain about the result. If your results are not what you would like, be honest enough with yourself to stop and look at what you are, or are not doing.

What advice have you been given that you are ignoring?

What advice have you been given that you are explaining away?

What are you not doing that you know you should be doing?

What are you doing that you know you shouldn't be doing?

You see, in all my years of coaching, I know that success is very often not the application of huge things or great secrets. It is the application of small, consistent actions, which lead to better results.

**Success is the application of small,
consistent actions which lead to better results.**

That's the good news! If you can improve one thing by a small percentage each week, you are guaranteed to improve your results. That's if you are working on the right things. Don't spend time shopping for the right display items, spend time improving your script for your presentation at the start of your party. Spend time reading or listening to CDs, which will help you develop your self-confidence. Learn how to improve your systems and your organisational skills. Make hostess-coaching and follow-up phone calls consistently part of your week. Ask every person at the party about joining the business. However, stop and listen to what they are saying before you ask. And it's helpful if you already know something about them before you ask.

For example, when they first turn up at the party and you take the time to get to know a bit about them, you may have started the conversation with the great open-ended question such as: "So, how do you know Susan?" They may have answered: "We go to play group together. I started only three months ago when I moved into this area, and Susan has really made an effort to help me get to know lots of people."

Hint — look at the difference in the following thinking to this information.

• Unsuccessful party plan people think that because she is new to the area, she won't know lots of people therefore would find it difficult to have parties — assumptions.

• Successful party plan people think that because she doesn't know lots of people the business would be great for her precisely because she would then be able to meet lots and lots of people.

Your next question may involve asking her about her family and what age they are, and where she has moved from and why. Now you have a foundation of information, which enables you to make a practical bid for her to consider joining the business. You're not guessing, you can talk to her in a way she can relate to. And she feels that you care about her because you have been asking open-ended questions.

Being Specific Is Powerful Persuasion

Please notice that when Jenny recruits Nicole, she doesn't talk about working around her kids' needs, she talks about being home for ***Jonathon*** and **Kim**. The more personal you make it, the more powerful it becomes. Don't talk about earning extra money, find out how much extra money she would like to earn per month and constantly use that specific amount, such as $1,400 a month, every time you talk about earning money. It's not earning money, it's not earning extra cash, it's not earning part-time, it's earning $1,400 a month, if that is her goal. In recruitment, the more specific your language is, the more powerful is the picture you're painting. And the stronger the Emotional Connection.

**The more specific your language is,
the more powerful is the picture you're painting.
And the stronger the Emotional Connection.**

Working around her kids' needs will not create such a strong and powerful picture for Nicole, as saying being home for Jonathon and Kim. She will have a strong Emotional Connection to this picture. This is why I would always be taking notes in a recruitment interview. You see, when people buy the products, they create a strong Emotional Connection to the products. When they decide to have a party, it may well be because they have a strong Emotional Connection to the product also. That is why they want to have a party, because they want to get some shoes or a bag you are selling for a discounted price, or even for free. But when you recruit, they seldom join because of an Emotional Connection to your product. They join because they have an Emotional Connection to something completely different, something other than your product. That is why recruiting is so much more difficult. You have to find out what that Emotional Connection is and then paint the picture of them achieving it, to make it stronger. But be warned, don't assume that they will join for the same reasons you did!

**They join because they have an Emotional Connection to something other than the product.
Don't assume that they will join for the same reasons you did!**

That would be too easy. You have to do your job and find out enough about them so you can discover what their Emotional Connection is, and then you know how to motivate them once they've joined.

Great Recruiting Tips

This has got to be one of the best techniques for closing the deal when you are recruiting. This idea was passed on to me by a friend who was extremely successful in party plan in several companies through the years. Whenever you recruit a new member, usually they love the product and assume that it will sell itself. They don't stop and think that they have to learn to sell. They assume the products do that for them. However, what is daunting to them, the biggest hurdle they believe they face, is the presentation. Standing up at the front of the room in a room full of strangers, is the one thing that makes most new people hesitate. And the most common question you will be asked is: "Do you think I can do that?" This is where their biggest doubt is, their biggest perceived hurdle. And what we tend to do is to go into reassurance mode. "Of course, you can do it. Look, if I could learn to do it, anyone can." And, of course, this means nothing to the person who is sitting there fearfully trying to imagine themselves getting up the courage to stand up in front of a room full of strangers. Your reassurance means nothing. You are already there, you look confident and professional. And if you are dealing with low self-esteem into the bargain, reassurance will not touch them at all. They'll simply not believe you. They'll think it's all right for you, etc.

So, how do you handle this question? "Do you think I can do that?" The answer is: "Do you think you can learn?"

When asked: "Do you think I can do that?"
The answer is: "Do you think you can learn?"

Most people believe they can learn, so the answer is usually yes. Once they have admitted that they think they could learn, look and see what has just happened! With that one yes, you have gained a new member.

In fact, if you're dealing with someone quite nervous or insecure, but who you know has great potential, get lots of yeses. Ask lots of questions. which will get a yes answer. "Do you love the products?"

"Do you enjoy helping other women feel good about themselves?"

"Would you like to earn some more money each month and still be home for Jonathon and Kim?"

It is far better to work towards closing the deal with lots of little yeses than it is to ask the big, daunting, terrifying question: "So, do you think you'd like to join the business?" It takes a very confident person to handle such a big question. Keep answering the little questions with lots of yeses and the final yes is much easier to get to. If you are dealing with someone who is not confident at the start, which is most people, using small yeses to lead them to join, is less likely to result in buyers' remorse and pulling back the next day.

How Do You Teach If You're Not Aware Of What You Do Well?

But, back to you. Developing your self-awareness is vital in building a team. If you don't know what you've been doing well, how are you going to teach them? If you don't analyse what you do and how well it works, how will you explain it to them? If you don't plan your week, they won't either. If you don't have the self-discipline and motivation to turn up to every training session, why should they? You have to become a role model for them. You have to walk the talk, do the doing and be the kind of person you would like them to become. Because while it's going to be fun having a team, at times it will be frustrating and they will be irritating. But they will be learning and they are going to learn from you. What are you going to change about yourself that you want them to become? Because growing a team no longer means you can slack off and let yourself off the hook. That will be letting your team down.

When you are goal-setting for yourself or for one of your team, there is an important concept to be aware of — Have, Do, Be. We really get this one the wrong way around. What we say is:

"If I <u>had</u> better customers, I would <u>do</u> lots of sales and I would <u>be</u> really successful." Have, Do, Be. Or, we say,

"If I <u>had</u> lots of money, I would <u>do</u> all the things wealthy people do and <u>be</u> really wealthy and..." Have, Do, Be.

But this is back to front. What we should be saying is:

"If I was to <u>become</u> the kind of person who attracts wealth, then I would <u>do</u> the things wealthy people do and <u>have</u> all the things a wealthy person has."

"If I <u>became</u> a great sales person, I would <u>do</u> the things successful sales people do and <u>have</u> lots of customers. Be, Do, Have.

What it always comes back to is you. It's what you become which is the catalyst for success. That's why whenever you set goals, you should always add, "How do I have to <u>be</u> in order to become the kind of person who has the ability to achieve my goals? This will tell you what you need to work on in order to achieve your goals. And if you identify specifically the skills and abilities you need and seriously work on becoming that kind of person, you will achieve your goal.

Review

It's time to review how far you've come. Look at what you've done well, whether you realised it or not at the time. Look at the total of your sales each month and think about what skills you've developed to achieve that level of sales. What have you been doing in the background of your business to achieve sales growth consistently? What awards and recognition have you got through the company? What skills and attributes have you developed to achieve this? It does not happen by accident! You actively did something to make it happen. Get clear on what you have been doing to make this happen.

After you have reviewed and done an inventory of your new skills and attributes, it's time to revisit your goals. Because your team is going to lift your revenue, you need to reset your goals much higher now. You need to set your goals for the whole team. Go back and review goal-setting if you have to, but this is the most dangerous time for most people. They have achieved more than they thought they could and they don't reset their goals. They lose focus, they stop being so disciplined and suddenly they find that they are no longer booking so many parties. They find they have lost motivation.

**Once they have achieved what they aimed for,
they have no idea what else they want after that.**

103

All this happens because they have not reset their goals. Once they have achieved what they aimed for, they have no idea what else they want after that. Or they feel that they should be grateful for what they already have. Sometimes it's difficult to set new goals when you have arrived at the one place you wanted to be. What now? What do you go for now? It's absolutely vital for your business that you reset your goals and make them bigger, so that they scare you a bit. But picture what your life would be like if you achieved these new goals. Breathtaking, isn't it. Go for it! Deep down you know you can do it.

This is usually the time when self-sabotage creeps in. When you have tasted success, this is the time that your "stuff" comes up. What thoughts are now racing through your mind about yourself and your business? What excuses are you starting to make? What discomfort are you starting to experience? I have coached so many people who tasted success then moved on. Suddenly for no good reason, things don't seem to be going right for them. There are a range of self-sabotaging behaviours such as moving from party plan company to party plan company, poor time management, focusing on the things that go wrong rather than all the things which go right, to name a few.

A Word On Loyalty

In mainstream business, when we are hired by a company, by default we owe them loyalty simply for the fact that they pay our wages. In exchange for wages, they expect a good day's work for a good day's pay. And they expect our loyalty. They expect that we will support them even when we are put in situations by angry customers who try to manipulate us to agree with them when they criticise the company. We are still expected to remain loyal.

When you join a party plan company, they lower the barriers of entry and try to make it as painless as possible for you to start up your own business. It costs a lot more to get into business normally, I can tell you. They offer you a great commission scheme and they offer great hostess gifts. They provide you with training, which is free and they heavily subsidise annual conference packages and offer amazing incentives such as international conference, cars and all sorts of lovely goodies.

And yet, in working within party plan over the years, I see very little loyalty to the party plan company, which supports its consultants so well. At the drop of a hat, people will turn and criticise, blackmail and manipulate their up-line and their Sales Manager. Some take it as a god-given right, that if I am part of this company, I have every right to complain, whinge and moan when I don't get what I want. In fact, it sometimes seems that the more successful they get, the more precious they get.

What has happened to gratitude and old-fashioned respect? Gratitude for all the things that this company is doing to support you in becoming successful. All the ways in which they lower the barriers so you can surge ahead despite not having large sums of money, despite not yet having the skills to run a successful business. They watch over you, they spend a lot of time thinking up incentives and they constantly seek to put specials together and products which they think will sell well — for you. All for you. They recognise that your success is their success. However, I don't often hear consultants recognise that the their success is dependent on the business success.

In mainstream business, you have no one who is supporting you in this manner. Conferences, either local or international are extremely expensive to get to, but many business people still attend because they know the value of what they can learn. Often, I've heard many party plan people actually criticise the company because they haven't made the package cheap enough. Quite frankly, if you haven't earned it, you don't deserve it.

I suggest that as you work your way through building your business, you look at what you are going to get out of it, rather than simply what it costs you. Look at value not cost. And the most successful people are not the ones with the highest sales, increased numbers of bookings or the best at recruitment. The most successful and greatest role models are the ones who remain humble and grateful for the opportunities they have been given. They are always respectful and never forget how they got to where they are. And always remember and appreciate the support they have had from their company, which has enabled them to achieve their success.

The Key To Greatness Is Gratitude

One of the secrets of success is gratitude. If you haven't watched *The Secret*, I would highly recommend that you do so. Gratitude for what you have already achieved will attract more of what you are grateful for. Do an assessment for all you have to be grateful for, on a monthly basis. We spend so much time focused on what we don't have, what we want to get, that we end up only seeing the negatives.

We have a life of striving for more. I'm not saying that aiming for targets and goals is a bad thing, it's certainly is not. But it should be balanced with gratitude for what we already have. Our families, our health, our great customers and the talents we have which have allowed us to get this far in the business. Make sure that at least once a month, you spend some time making a list of things to be grateful for. While it seems unnecessary to say, treat

NOTES

NOTES

NOTES

13

It's Just Business

Jenny was fuming. One of her best customers had ordered a second bag for her daughter. It was top of the range and one of the most expensive, a repeat of the one she had bought for herself. She'd loved the bag and had shown it to her daughter who wanted one the same. Jenny had ordered it only to be told it was being discontinued from the range. She loved this bag and had sold a few despite it being one of the most expensive in the range, so she was puzzled as to why they would be not producing it any more.

"This doesn't make sense," she complained to Sandra at their next training meeting. "It's not as if it's not a good seller. Why would they stop selling something which is selling well?"

Sandra looked around the group. "How many of you have sold that bag?" One lady put her hand up. "I've sold one."

Sandra looked at Jenny, "That's probably why. It's selling but not well enough. The new range will be out soon. Try selling one of the new set to her." And Sandra continued with her meeting.

But Jenny wasn't satisfied. "Sandra, can you ask head office if they will reconsider?"

"It won't make a difference, Jenny. They've made their decision."

"But I can sell more of those bags," Jenny was determined not to be put off.

"I'll find out why they're discontinuing it from the range for you, but I don't think they will change their mind. But I'll ask. Okay? Now, can we get on with the meeting?"

Jenny felt like Sandra hadn't taken it seriously enough and, at the break, wandered outside to get away from all the positive thinking and optimism that was floating around the meeting. She was still unhappy about not being able to sell that bag. Outside, a couple of women were smoking and she noticed that their discussion ceased as she walked out the door.

"Hi, I'm Stella. I noticed you had an argument with Sandra. So, tell me, are you happy with being in her team? Or are you like us, and have just about had enough?"

Jenny was surprised and didn't quite know what to say. "It wasn't really an argument. It's just I've got an order for a bag they've decided to discontinue. It's so stupid, why would they discontinue something that is selling so well? And to be honest, it felt a bit as if Sandra slid over it. She didn't take it all that seriously."

"Actually, we know how you feel 'cos we're not real happy with Sandra either. We only started two months ago and Sandra has been spending a lot of time with two newbies who started after us. We don't think she's giving us enough support."

"Well," said Jenny, a bit taken aback, "have you asked her for more support?"

"Yes, but she just gives us stuff to do then moves on. We'd like a bit more support."

"I'm thinking of leaving if I don't get more support," said her friend as she stubbed out her cigarette. "Or at least see if I can switch teams. I'd like to be in Peggy's team. She's great, they have great fun in their training sessions."

"Can you do that?" Jenny was surprised, she hadn't heard of anybody switching teams.

"Well, it depends on how flexible they want to be if they want to keep their people. I guess we'll find out, won't we?"

Jenny felt a bit disloyal and glanced over her shoulder. "Looks like they're starting again. We'd better go in."

"Hey, do you want to meet for coffee?" Stella walked beside her. "We could have a chat about some of the changes we want to see."

"Sure, give me a call." Jenny gave her a business card with her phone number on it and returned to her seat. She didn't feel right about the conversation, but now she watched closely as Sandra continued on with the training. Had she been looking at Sandra through rose-tinted lenses? Had she been getting as much support as she should have? Were there better teams within the company that would help her become more successful? Jenny watched through narrowed eyes as Sandra congratulated a new achiever.

Two days later, Jenny's anger and frustration erupted again. Martina was a very difficult customer. So when her order finally arrived after being delayed for a range of reasons, all problems with J'Adore's systems, it was the wrong bag and shoes. Jenny phoned through the changes and then had to phone Martina and tell her that the order would be at least another week. Martina complained bitterly and unfortunately Jenny didn't have this set in her size in her kit to give her in the meantime. As if she'd take them anyway, Jenny thought to herself. She suspected the woman simply liked lording it over everyone else. She lived in a bit of a mansion on the river, travelled internationally on a frequent basis with her husband, and quite frankly, was not the kind of person Jenny would chose as a friend. Sure enough, Martina didn't hold back and tore strips off Jenny first before she turned her attention to the company. She threatened to cancel the order as she had wanted to take them with her on her next trip. She was leaving the day after tomorrow. Her order would be arriving too late. Jenny apologised, heard her out and apologised again.

She phoned Sandra to see if she could pull any strings to get it sent out sooner. "Sorry kid, nothing I can do. You know, mistakes happen. Not too often, thank goodness, but she's just going to have to wait. Did you apologise to her?"

"Only three times so far," Jenny said bitterly. "She's threatening to cancel her order. What can I do?"

"Let her," replied Sandra.

"What!" Jenny couldn't believe her ears. "What, refund her money and let her walk away!"

"If she can't understand about a simple mistake, she's not going to be a great customer to have any way. I'd let her go if she wants to walk."

"But that would be two customers I'd have lost this week," objected Jenny. "I feel like I'm bringing them in, making sales, and the company is driving them away." She watched Sandra to see her reaction.

"Well, you win some, you lose some. When you deal with more customers as your business grows, you can't keep them all happy. You've going to lose some. And some aren't worth keeping. Get over it."

Jenny spent the rest of the day in a rage. It was just too much! She slammed the fridge door. She had worked so hard to get her sales up and to start recruiting. And J'Adore were doing this to her. "It's as if they were deliberately doing things to her to stop her earning more money," she muttered under her breath. Shocked, she stopped and thought about it. No, she was just unlucky. But what if she wasn't? She thought again about what Stella had said. And again she could feel her temper rising. Sandra definitely hadn't taken her seriously. She virtually said to let the customer walk away. She thought about that for a while. Martina was difficult and demanding. But she was loaded. Jenny didn't want her to walk away. She wanted Martina to spend lots more money with her.

She was still see-sawing when Mark arrived home after making a round of deliveries for her. He'd started doing the deliveries for her to leave her free to spend more time hostess coaching and focusing on Nicole, her new team member.

"Gosh, that Leigh is a dag," he chuckled. "She was so excited to get her shoes, you should have seen her prancing around the kitchen in them. She's nuts!"

"Who cares as long as she buys from us," responded Jenny. "At least we were able to give her what she wanted."

"Helloooo" Mark looked at her speculatively. "What's happened? What's going on?" Jenny told him about the situation with Martina. "Sandra thinks that if she threatens to cancel, I should let her. That she's more trouble than she's worth."

"And is she?" Mark took a drink from the fridge and leaned against the bench, watching her.

"She's loaded! She's going to buy lots from me. I don't want to walk away from her. I don't think that if a customer is difficult, you should just simply let them go."

"I guess it all depends on the customer. And it depends on why you have her for a customer." Mark added.

"What do you mean?" Now he had her attention.

"Well, are you just in this business for yourself? Or do you truly want to give customers what they want? What I like about when you started, was that you wanted to build their self-confidence. You wanted them to feel better about themselves. You wanted to add a bit of style to their lives. If I remember rightly, that was what excited you about this company. It was the women's reaction to the shoes and the bags. Real Italian style at prices they could afford. Since when did it change to 'I need to keep them so I can make lots of money from them?'"

Jenny frowned. "Well, it hasn't really. But I have targets to meet now," she said slowly, trying to think this through. Mark was right in what he was saying, but she knew that if she could keep Martina happy, she would get a lot of business from her.

"So," Mark summarised, "there's been a change. Now you're saying that you'll do anything to keep every customer, no matter how they treat you, no matter how disrespectful they are of you, no matter how much they waste your time and look how much time we've spent just discussing her so far! As long as she keeps buying, that's the most important thing."

"Well, no." Jenny could see the sense of what he was saying. "In an ideal world, you would walk away from people like her, but I want to reach my targets."

"At any cost? Are you going to deal with any customers regardless of how they treat you?"

"Of course not!" Jenny was getting a bit sick of this conversation. "Anyway, it's not so much Martina who has annoyed me, actually it's Sandra. I don't think she's as supportive as I originally thought. She didn't seem to take the discontinued line very seriously. I felt a bit dismissed. She told me to get over it! And I met these two ladies who are ready to leave because of Sandra. I'm not sure anymore about her."

Mark took another drink. "Have you talked to her about your doubts?"

"No, I thought I should make up my mind first then say something to her."

"Is that the business way to do things? Is that you being honest and open so she can support you?"

"You think I should go and talk to her?"

"She's your upline, she's there to support you. I seem to remember you telling someone else this. If you don't talk to her she just assumes that everything thing is okay. If I were you, I'd nip this in the bud and get it out in the open rather than letting it fester." He started to walk away, and called over his shoulder: "And I wouldn't be mixing with those two who are thinking about leaving. Sounds to me like they are stirring the pot. Not very motivating types to be around."

Jenny took her coffee and sat outside to think. What had happened? She had got frustrated when two things happened at once. Was this just business? Was Sandra right? The more customers you got, did the number of problems increase in proportion also? Was this the next set of skills she had to learn? Handling difficult customers, changes within the company without the frustration ruining her day? How did you learn to do that? Jenny picked up her mobile phone and called Sandra. She was going to make a time to meet and discuss this whole thing with her.

Mark came out and sat down across the table in the pergola with her. "Where are you at? Still thinking about leaving? That's a big decision."

"I guess I'm still sore at them taking out that set. I have customers who love that bag. I could sell more." She was so sure about this. How could the company get it so wrong?

"Listen to me." He spoke softly but firmly. "No matter how much they love that bag, one or two customers do not make a trend. Even if it feels like it to you. They have to make business decisions. One customer request does not make a trend. It just seems like it to you."

Jenny didn't comment but she still didn't feel happy.

"Go back and revisit your goals," he suggested. "Refocus. Remember what you are doing this for. You've been putting the ground work in for a while now and whether you realise it or not, it's starting to gain momentum. It's not quite as hard work as it was. Your business is really starting to take off. Don't go all emotional on me now. I was just starting to wonder how long it would be before I gave up my job and helped you in yours."

Jenny gasped. "Are you for real?"

"Well, think about it. Look how much running around you do. Picking up orders, posting returns, banking and deliveries to name just a few. If you were able to spend more time with your team instead of this running around, you'd increase your revenue. I was thinking about approaching my boss and suggesting that I pull back to part-time. He won't be happy, but it would be interesting to see how it impacted on your business. But if you're going to leave…"

"Oh, Mark! Of course I'm not going to leave. And it would be wonderful if you could do all the running around for me! I can't believe you are even suggesting it. That would give me so much more time. Thank you!" And she raced around the table to give him a big hug.

Jenny wasn't very comfortable on her way to meet Sandra. She didn't quite know what to say but she had found a book on handling difficult conversations and had practised the techniques suggested. She would stick to the subject and explain how she felt without actually accusing Sandra of anything. That way Sandra wouldn't feel attacked and they would have an effective conversation where they could clear the air. According to the book!

Once they had settled with a coffee and chatted for a while, Jenny broached the subject. "Sandra, I wanted to talk to you because there are a couple of things I wanted to get off my mind." She started.

"I'm glad you did, if you hadn't called me I would've called you."

"Really?" Jenny was a bit taken aback. "Why?"

"Well, I know you've had a couple of knockbacks lately and I saw you talking to Stella, and that's not going to make you feel any better."

Jenny was surprised. She's never heard Sandra being other than positive about people in her team. She decided to tread carefully. "Why would you say that?"

"Well, I have given her so much support but I'm not going to do the work for her. Stella is one of those people who wants to "have been" successful. She doesn't want to put in the hard work, but she wants the good results. She's lazy and she's negative. In fact, I would go as far to say that she almost infects people around her." Sandra stopped and looked out the window for a moment. "It's been really hard but I finally gave her some things to do and if she doesn't do them, I'm washing my hands of her. But in the meantime, she's getting to as many people as she can, and she's spreading quite unsettling stuff."

"I had no idea," said Jenny, "I can see what you mean. Is this what it's like? Running a team?" She was horrified at the thought of handling this type of person.

"Sometimes." Sandra smiled. "Although, most of the time it's dealing with people who are doing their best. And every now and again, you find a star. Someone who tries everything you teach them, and just soars. You're one of my stars, you know Jenny."

"Who, me?"

"Yes, you. I'm so proud of you. You've worked so hard. You've got Nicole now and you're on your way. I expect to see you and Mark at conference. And your team will grow in no time. It's been really rewarding watching your progress."

Jenny didn't know what to say. She took a sip of coffee to give her time to think. She felt an absolute cow. Sandra had supported her in the best way possible. She hadn't smothered her, she had allowed her the space to grow and make her own mistakes. But she had always been there for her.

"I think I owe you an apology, Sandra, I've been so unhappy with the company, and I must admit that I wasn't too happy with you either at one stage. When we discussed the bag, which was discontinued, I felt quite dismissed. I felt that you…"

"I know, I'm sorry about that, " Sandra interrupted her. "I'd just been speaking to Stella and I'd just about had enough of emotional women for one night. And yes, I was a bit short with you. But I thought you'd be fine. You'd handle it. You're so sensible and not likely to allow things to fester. I knew if you weren't happy, you'd come to me and we'd talk about it. But I've been so busy, I forgot. I'm sorry."

Jenny smiled. "Just one more lesson on the pathway to success," she said. "I left it a bit late to talk to you about it all anyway. So partly my fault also. But tell me, do you really think I should let Martina go?"

"Jenny, you deserve the respect of your customers. Don't let them bully you into feeling bad about yourself, your business or J'Adore. It's a bit like having Stella for a customer. You want to allow them to move on. You know that you do the best you can for them. If they don't appreciate it, apologise and move on. We're all grown-ups here. If they can't handle a bit of a disappointment without taking it out on you, I wouldn't want them in my circle." She took a sip of coffee. "And one last thing. It's great to be passionate about J'Adore and the products. It's great to be passionate about helping your customers. But you must not forget that you are in business now. There are lots of reasons as to why business decisions are made. You have to have faith that the decisions the company make are ultimately the best thing for you and your business. You need to step back a bit, Jenny."

"That's what Mark says," she admitted. "I'll try. And I'll have a think about what you've said about Martina. You know, now I think about it, that was exactly what I did with Sarah, I walked away and left her to do her business her way. I can see now that I need to do that in other areas of my life. Friends, customers, perhaps even with some of the family. I can't believe the impact Stella had on me with that one short conversation. Unbelievable. What a lesson this has been. Timely too, as I grow my team." Jenny grinned. " I got another two inquiries about the business at last night's party," she announced.

"Good for you! See? I said you had cracked it."

"One last thing, Sandra. How's Sarah going? I haven't seen her at training for a while and we haven't kept in touch. She left me a message that she was going to stop with the party plan."

Sandra didn't hold back. "I think we're going to lose her, Jenny. She has the strongest comfort zone and doesn't want to do things our way. She was going to take on the world, get to every international conference, but I couldn't even get her to learn the presentation." Sandra shook her head in frustration. "I've given her all the support I can, but she's fighting me all the way. Unfortunately, I think she's on the way out. Even though she has the potential to do so well."

"I tried to help her, too. It's so sad. I felt so bad when I consciously made the decision to stop supporting her until she stepped up to the mark herself."

"Wait till you have to take that approach with one of your own team!" Sandra chuckled.

"No! None of my team is going to be like that. They're going to have the best training, the best support. They're going to be little rockets!"

Jenny and Sandra were still chuckling when they left the coffee shop. Neither saw Sarah watching them from the doorway of one of the nearby shops.

14

Coaching For Business Perspective

When emotions are running high, thinking is running low, is an old saying. In fact, if you've learnt about emotional intelligence, you'll know that when you get highly emotional, your brain stops thinking altogether and you simply react. Which is why some people do things that are out of character while under extreme stress, such as road rage or physical abuse. As women, our emotions can be like a roller-coaster. We are emotional beings. We feel very protective towards our customers and will charge in to fight to get them justice if we think that something is unfair. We are passionate about our business. Usually we don't approach it in a cool, logical manner. We care!

We are passionate about our business.
Usually we don't approach it in a cool, logical manner.
We care!

So when something goes wrong, we immediately go into high drive emotionally and in this state, we don't get all the facts. We take what we hear as gospel and are likely to make poor business decisions. And, sometimes when the emotions are running high, we are unlikely to listen to logic, even when the facts are presented to us. In reality, it takes a cool head to become Sales Manager of a party plan company.

In business, you want to base your decisions on facts, not feelings. Yet again, I say, how you are feeling is not an indication of how you are doing. Your results are the only indication of how you are doing. If something goes wrong for one of your customers, yes, get frustrated, that's normal. It's all about being a human being and caring about your customer. But business has a much bigger focus than just one or two customers. It has a much longer time horizon than your end-of-month results. Think about it for a moment. If a business has thousands and thousands of customers, it certainly does want to keep them happy. But if only a few of those customers love a product, if that product is no longer profitable because the supplier adds a significant price increase or that particular product becomes difficult to get, then no matter how much one or two customers love it, it is no longer profitable for the company to offer it for sale. Now I'm not saying that a company should chop and change all the time, but often when one of our customers feels let down, we assume the business does not care. This is simply not true in most cases. And as you grow your business, you are going to have to explain things to your customers that you are not happy with, but you have to support the company and trust that it is doing what is good for its customers in the long run.

As women, one of the things we have to learn is to stand back and look at our business so we can respond, rather than react emotionally. You must base your conclusions and your decisions on fact, not emotion. When you hear something which results in your feeling any strong emotion at all — frustration, a sense of injustice, anger or any other emotion for yourself or on behalf of another — you must stop and find out all the information before you respond. Do not react before you have heard the other side of the story!

When you hear something, which makes
you feel frustrated
or feel a sense of injustice for others,
you must stop and find out all the information
before you respond.
Do not react before you have heard
the other side of the story!

I have seen more party plan success go down the drain because they were diving in to address a problem on behalf of someone else. Their strong emotion for that person totally distracts them from their own business and I've even seen some people leave the company because of "perceived" injustices to others. The business response is always to get all the information before you decide how you are going to respond. Do not react, decide how you are going to respond. Whether it be a customer who is unhappy for some reason, or someone who has confided in you about some problems they are having with an individual/their team/their upline/the company. Remember, the phrase is: "So, what are you going to do about it?" The fact of the matter is this, you can't fix this problem for them. Only they can fix their problems. For example, if they are not getting on with someone else, they need to approach that person, suggest they have a coffee and try to sort it out between them. You can't fix it for them. The best thing you can do, the most supportive thing you can do and the only ethical thing to do, is to coach them to solve their problems themselves.

Your Stats

This is why you need to keep track of your dollars and your statistics. You'll have some months where your family are going through "stuff", your friends' marriages are breaking up, you've put on a bit of weight and you feel you're just not getting anywhere. And you'll exceed your targets! Other months, you'll be flying high, you'll be full of energy and you'll have that one party which did so well in sales and bookings, and yet you'll fall short of your target. How you feel is not an indicator of how you are doing.

How you feel is not an indicator of how you are doing!
Complaining is like taking a stress pill,
you feel better but nothing has changed.

Your Statistics Are Your Training Indicator

I can't stress enough how important it is to keep track of your stats. Get into the habit of starting each month with setting your goals, and ending your month with a long hard look at your "actuals". This will tell you how you are going. This is the time you absolutely have to face your results and be totally honest with yourself. How many parties did you have? What were the sales at each one? What are your average sales? How many bookings did you get? How many cancellations did you get? How many people did you recruit? Don't cringe from these, they will tell you what you need to learn!

Your stats will tell you what you need to learn to do better.
They are your training guide.

If you did the same number of parties as the month before but your sales average was less than the month before, check your presentation at the start of the party. Did you do less hostess coaching? What did you do differently? Find that and you find the key to increasing your sales. Are you starting to take short-cuts? Sometimes, when we have done the presentation over and over, we get a bit sick of ourselves. But remember, at each party it is the first time that your guests have heard you.

You see, it's not the type of people who come to parties that influence the sales. And it's not the neighbourhood. It's you. I know without a shadow of a doubt that if we put someone who was doing very well into your parties, your sales would increase. Find out what you need to be better at, and get yourself along to training and learn from the best. The more frequently you are prepared to look at the numbers, the faster you will improve. If you are always looking the other way and hoping things will get better, your learning will be like pushing .... up hill. And we get enough of that in our lives without doing it to ourselves in our business as well.

The Barnyard Versus The Schoolyard

If we can, we will try and find shortcuts. You see there is a concept called The Barnyard versus The Schoolyard. It is a great lesson to keep this in mind for ourselves and especially when you start to train your team. The reality is that we learn some life lessons which come back to bite us in the real world. It goes like this. The objective at school is to pass exams. So we can muck around all year and then cram like crazy for the last few weeks, and still pass your exams. You learned a lot but you'll forget it just as quickly. You've not gained knowledge and you've not got any wisdom, but you passed the exam. You got a qualification but it's questionable whether you got an education. The law of the Schoolyard is a quick-fix shortcut. And it leaves us with the impression that we can take this approach elsewhere in our lives.

However, in natural laws, this doesn't work. When it comes to natural systems such as the farm, success, your body or your business, they are all governed by natural laws and principles. You know that if you wanted to become fitter, doing 50 push-ups is not going to get you there. You know you have to train. Your body responds to the natural law of the Farmyard.

Imagine for a moment if you were on a farm and you had forgotten to plant your crop. It would do you no good if you raced around, bought seed, planted it and watered it in the expectation that you would have a crop in no time flat. You have to follow the natural laws and clear the land at the right time, fertilise the soil, plant at the right time and water the right amount at the right time. Then when the time is right, the seeds will grow into a healthy crop. which you will harvest, again at the right time. This is the Farmyard law. You can't take shortcuts. You can't fake it. And a business is also a natural system. So are relationships. You can't build a relationship on a smile, it has to go deeper than that. You can't fake it or take shortcuts if you want a long-term relationship. And it's the same with your business. You have to plan what you are going to do.

You have to learn new skills and instil self-discipline. You have to become more organised. And still it's not going to happen overnight. It is a natural system with natural laws and principles. So if you expect to build a business within the first couple of months, you'd better get real and think again. The law of the farm is a harvest. The law of the schoolyard is a quick, short-term fix. Be honest with yourself. Be real. And help your team do the same. Set your expectations to the reality of the task ahead of you and you will experience less frustration, less disappointment and less of an emotional roller-coaster.

Beware the OPP Virus!

Do not get wrapped up in Other People's Problems! It is so easy to chat about what you are not satisfied with, but it's so difficult to stay impartial when that person is emotional. We care, and as women, we are naturally nurturing. Whether they are frustrated, angry or disillusioned, don't become infected by their emotion. This will impact your attitude and the results of your business faster than you can say: "That's not fair!" You do not know the full story behind what is happening. You are only hearing one version. And for all you know, it may well be that the company would willingly let this person walk away because of all the emotional turmoil she creates around her.

It is difficult enough to keep yourself focused and motivated, without a "friend" dragging you down with her problems and her frustration. Did you know that emotion is contagious? And the person with the strongest emotion infects everyone around them — even when they have not said a word. Experiments have been done in waiting rooms where people have sat in silence, waiting for their appointments. If one person is experiencing a strong emotion, either happiness or anger, without saying a word they infect every other person sitting in that room. If it can happen without words, imagine what a negative, whinging discussion can have on you!

No Pity Parties!

If you are serious about building your business, don't get caught up in other people's problems. Help them deal with their problems by asking:

"So, what are *you* going to do about it?"

Don't sympathise. You can empathise but sympathy feeds self-pity. And you want to avoid all Pity Parties. No Pity Parties! Suggest she go and talk to her upline and discuss the whole subject. The fact of the matter is that if she can't talk to her upline, she doesn't have a good relationship with her. That's what your upline is for, to support, train and mentor you through problems. She should be the first person you talk to when you have a problem. When people complain to you, or you find yourself complaining, try to get them to be honest with themselves. What have they done that has contributed to this situation? If they have done nothing, such as having a very demanding customer who got the wrong order, stop and think about the most professional businesswoman you know or know of, and ask yourself, what would she do in this situation? How would she respond to this? Would she find a way to release her frustration (not on her family, friends or the cat!), and then would she just get on with things? She wouldn't wallow in the emotion of frustration and involve all her friends and anyone else who will listen to her also in the Pity Party.

And if you're not happy with the company for one reason or another, you need to stop and think things through before you say anything to anyone. Complaining is like taking a stress pill, you feel better but nothing has changed. If you have any doubts or questions about why the company does anything, the person to discuss this with is your upline. She'll know why these things are happening and she'll be able to give you the full business picture.

Keeping Customer Records For Repeat Sales

Whether you keep a database on computer files or cards in a box, which you carry in your car with you, if you want repeat sales you need to keep accurate records of your customers. What did they buy? What colour was it? Was there a special request? Have they had any special events in their lives such as a new baby? Or has one of their children started school? If their youngest has started school and they have been a hostess, they have good potential for recruiting. Yes, their children have started school and they will now be starting to think about what they are going to do with their time. They are starting to get their lives back. And if they already love the product enough to have a couple of parties, you should follow-up with a recruiting bid.

If you keep records, you will know a month ahead whether they, or their family have birthdays coming up or a time which you can make a suggestion for having a party. Prepare a letter and every month go through your cards to see who has birthdays the following month. Then follow-up the letter with a phone call suggesting that they have a party so they can either get the hostess gift for themselves, or for their family. Remember, Valentine's Day, wedding anniversaries, new product launches (you should be able to go to all your previous hostesses at least twice a year with these!). Christmas, school holidays, Mother's Day, Father's Day, there are any number of reasons to go back to your Hostesses to encourage them to hold another party. Try to get yourself into the rhythm of doing a minimum of two to three parties a year per hostess. When you speak with them, plant the seed and tell them that you like to keep in touch at least three or four times a year.

Is that okay or would they prefer for you to get back in touch sooner? Don't assume that your contact is going to be a nuisance. There may be something coming up which having a party would get them products they will be needing by a certain date.

Don't assume that your contact is going to be a nuisance.

Remember to tempt them with word pictures of what is on offer and don't forget to do your hostess coaching even if she has had a party before. Send her extra catalogues so she can take outside orders. She may not remember what she did last time that worked so well.

If you have the kind of product that generates repeat business, you need to stay on top of your records so you can follow up. Service calls, such as replacing split seals, wrong sizing, wrong colour make-up can all lead to new parties, if you take advantage of the opportunity. I have heard about people who have built a whole new business after moving to a new town, by simply doing service calls and turning them into parties. A complaint is always an opportunity.

You can apologise, replace the product and then make them an overly generous offer as a hostess to make up for the inconvenience. While the company will offer a hostess gift, you can add value by adding to that hostess gift. Stop and think for a moment. It might cost you a bit for an extra hostess gift, but what sales might you make if she has a party. Sometimes an extra hostess gift is worth creating as an incentive. However, a word of warning. It is important to monitor what you are spending in your business to make sure that you are profitable. There's no point being in business to break even. You do not want to spend all that time and effort only to break even. Your goal is not just to get to international conference and build a team but to have a profitable business.

NOTES

NOTES

NOTES

15

Growing Your Team

Jenny's team had grown to three. It was satisfying to be able to share her learning with these women who were new to party plan and so hungry to learn. She so wanted them to be successful and just thinking about their potential, excited her. She wanted to show them the full potential of what they could build for themselves. So her first move was a one-on-one session with each of them to find out what their goals and ambitions were. She needed to understand why they had joined party plan. She knew enough to understand that probably they would have completely different reasons from why she had joined. But she needed to know what their Emotional Connection was to, so she could keep them focused and motivated. As she headed out the door to have her second meeting with Nicole, she was humming to herself and thinking about the new outfits she needed to buy for the Hawaiian conference. While she only had a small team, her sales had reached her targets easily.

At the coffee shop, her heart sank when she saw the look on Nicole's face. "What's wrong?" she asked as she sat down. "You look as if something terrible has happened."

Nicole looked close to tears. "I tried, but it didn't work. I'm sorry." Her bottom lip quivered.

Quickly, Jenny jumped in, "Listen, how about I get us both a coffee and we'll have a chat about it? Whatever it is. I'm sure there's nothing so bad we can't find a way through it." While she waited in the queue, Jenny prepared herself to hold back her reaction to whatever it was that Nicole was going to tell her. She remembered Mark's advice, "Business women respond, they don't react!"

When she returned to the table, Nicole had her composure under control but still looked down in the mouth. "Now, how about you tell me what's wrong. And take your time." Jenny didn't want to have to cope with a sobbing woman. She couldn't imagine what could possibly have happened.

"I tried, you know, making the calls. But I don't think this is right for me. It didn't work. Nothing worked," she wailed. "My husband was right, I'm hopeless at this." She hiccuped over her coffee.

Jenny just stopped herself in time. She almost said, Oh, is that all? But that would have undermined the importance of what Nicole was feeling. Before she could say anything, Nicole continued. "It's all right for you. You're really confident and you know what you are doing. I feel dreadful, I don't know what to say, I don't want to be pushy. And I don't really see why they should do me a favour by having a party."

Jenny froze. Here was an echo from the past. It was like talking to Sarah all over again. She was stunned and for a moment she wasn't sure what to say. She took a sip of coffee to buy some time. What had happened to the confident, excited Nicole? In fact, that was a good question. She proceeded gently. "Nicole, what's happened? You were so enthusiastic the other day, you were dying to get started. What happened?"

Nicole hung her head. "Well for starters, my husband is what happened. Any idea he gets is a good one. Any idea I get of earning money or making my way in the world, he laughs at. He says I'll be hopeless at it."

Jenny knew she had to proceed very carefully. She didn't want to put Nicole's husband down (the sod!) but she wanted to help Nicole regain her confidence. "Nicole, maybe he finds it a bit threatening when you try something new. Maybe he's a bit frightened that you will be good at it. It might make him feel a bit insecure." Idiot! She thought. "Perhaps it's time to put aside what he's been saying, and just give it a try,"

"I tried. I made the phone calls and I don't have one booking." Her chin wobbled again.

"Well, let's see what you said. So firstly, how many calls did you make?"

"Lots. And I didn't get one booking!"

"How many is lots," Jenny persisted.

Nicole stopped and counted on her fingers. "I phoned Sharon, my sister-in-law, Beck, my neighbour, and Angie from mother's group. Three, I made three calls."

"Three calls." Jenny stopped herself from adding, only three calls. "And what was the reason they turned you down?"

Nicole took a deep breath. "Sharon's going down south next week, so she's too busy."

"Did you suggest you'd call her when she got back?" Jenny was feeling a bit impatient. She'd never been into Pity Parties. She always just shook things off and got on with it. Except the time she sobbed all over Mark's shoulder, she reminded herself.

"Beck has just had a baby and didn't really think she could cope. And

Angie's baby has a bad cold and she said she couldn't think about it at the moment."

"But that's great news. That's not three rejections." Jenny had brightened up considerably. If only she could get Nicole to see what she could see. "You've not had three nos. You've had three not nows." She smiled at Nicole and was delighted when she received a hesitant smile back. "Did you bring your diary with you?"

Nicole reached into the backpack she always carried and pulled out a large black diary. Jenny found herself wondering why Nicole never used a handbag.

"Good girl. Now open it up and write down when you are going to make each of these women a follow-up phone call. And we'll go through what you can say to them together. And while we're at it, let's just review what you are saying on the phone."

By the time they had had their second cup of coffee, Nicole had brightened right up. But Jenny had one more thing she wanted to say. "Nicole, about your husband. Many people think they know us and when we step out of our comfort zones, it scares them a bit. It may well be that your husband feels much more secure if he thinks he knows what you're good at. Perhaps you should sit down and talk to him about this new business you've started," Jenny said rather pointedly.

"I tried the other day, but he just talks over me and laughs at me. Tells me how stupid I am." At least Nicole was making eye contact with Jenny now.

Jenny smiled. "You know something, my husband didn't want to know when I first started. I remember when I first told him I'd joined, he was furious that I'd spent the money and when I tried to talk to him about it, he just turned the TV up."

Nicole's eye's widened. "Really? What happened?"

"He changed his tune fast enough when I started making sales. He couldn't believe how much I sold in my first couple of parties. He sat up and took notice then," Jenny said with satisfaction. "And I'll let you into a little secret. He's thinking about going part-time with his job so he can help me with my business. No-one pays for him and me to go to Hawaii where he works." Jenny suddenly realised how far she and Mark had come together and her heart went out to Nicole. She remembered the anguish of forcing yourself to make the phone calls, the awkwardness of approaching complete strangers at parties, of dreading those first few moments in the limelight at the start of the party. She so wanted to support Nicole through these fears.

"Nicole, about your husband, in the cold light of day, there are two possibilities here and the both involve choice on your part. No one can make these decisions for you," she reached across the table and squeezed Nicole's hand, "And no-one has the right to judge you for whatever decisions you make."

"Your husband sounds nice but I can't see mine changing his mind. What are the decisions?" Nicole asked quietly.

"Firstly, you must do everything in your power to win your husband over. We know that those who have the full support of their partners are more likely to be successful. There are enough things to deal with internally to get past, without having to fight someone in your family at the same time. Firstly, try to talk to him and I'll show you a format that has worked well. If that doesn't work, just keep your head down and get your first couple of parties under your belt. Maybe your sales will change his mind. However, if for some reason, he does not support you and continues his verbal abuse," Jenny hesitated to let the full impact of her words to sink in, "you're going to have to decide whether you'll pull back and continue in the relationship as it is. Or whether you will plough ahead, keep trying to win him over but continue on the pathway, which is best for you. Despite what he says."

Nicole sat thinking for a while. When she raised her head, she looked at Jenny and Jenny could hear the quiet determination in her voice. "I'll do what you suggest. I'll try again but I don't think he'll change his mind. He doesn't like it when I get ideas. And he says that you're putting stupid ideas into my head. That I'm stupid for listening to you. But I'm going to do this. This is my chance and I want to do it."

Jenny felt tears prickle in her eyes. She'd heard stories of great courage in her life, but she recognised real courage when she saw it. Nicole believed that her partner of 10 years was not going to accept her business. But she was going to proceed on her own pathway regardless. Jenny couldn't even imagine what she was going to have to face and experience to get past this and her heart went out to her.

"Nicole, I'll be there for you all the way, but if you choose this pathway, you're going to have to start making those calls. You need to focus on getting bookings." She leaned forward in earnest. "Nicole, I have absolute faith in you, I know you can do this if you put your mind to it."

Nicole gave a small smile. "Jenny, I know you'll say that to all your team. But I appreciate you supporting me. I am going to give this my best shot. I think this is my chance. If I don't take this, my life will be unbearable. I'll never be able to try anything again."

"You just let me know what you are going to do, what you need from me and I'll be there for you. But I can't help you with your husband. You're going to have to handle that situation. But you can call me anytime. I'll help anyway I can."

As they parted, Jenny added one last piece of advice. "Remember, don't ask people to have a party. Describe the shoes and bags to them, tell them how much fun the party will be and ask them to support you by having a party."

Jenny's meeting with Nicole was almost the opposite of her latest recruit, Charlene. Charlene was determined, confident and hungry to learn. She had done her calls and already had five parties in the pipeline. "I want to pay for my kids to go to private school," she said when Jenny asked her why she was joining. "I left school before I finished high school and my first job was in Coles. I want my kids to have the best education and so does my husband. They've got a few years to go yet, but that gives me time to build a fund. I want them to go to private school."

Jenny was awestruck. Charlene was a shining example of what it means to be focused and determined. Her Emotional Connection was so strong. Jenny knew she'd have no trouble getting Charlene to training each month. Charlene was going to be what Jenny now thought of as a low-maintenance lady. Mentally, she rated her team by the level of support they required. Charlene was low maintenance, whereas Nicole was going to be on-going high maintenance for a while. And who knows what was going to happen for her. By joining a party plan business she was facing serious obstacles in self-esteem to begin with. A disapproving partner was the pits. It magnified your self-doubt just at the time you needed confidence the most. And Jenny was now convinced, that when women first start to discover their potential, it was often a catalyst which brought relationship issues to the surface — to be handled and addressed or avoided, as the case may be. She was still deep in thought when her front door bell rang. Opening the door, Jenny took one look and gasped, "Sarah!"

"Can I come in?" Sarah stepped forward and as she passed Jenny, she turned and gave her a big hug. Jenny was still trying to recover from the surprise. As she wrapped her arms around Sarah, she realised how much she missed their sessions. Their crazy planning, the things that used to make them laugh, just the plain sharing of it.

"Come in. It's so good to see you."

"I saw you and Sandra together at the coffee shop. You looked so close, so intense. I realised how much I missed our friendship. I just decided it was time to reconnect. I hope you're okay with it?" Sarah looked so hesitant. Jenny couldn't stop herself from grinning. "Idiot. Of course it's okay. I'm delighted you're here. I've missed you."

"I'm not interrupting your hostess coaching or anything like that, am I?" Apparently, Sarah couldn't resist a dig.

"Well, yes actually, you are. But it's worth it. What have you been up to? Bring me up to date."

"Actually, the reason I'm here is because of seeing you and Sandra yesterday. You seemed to have such a bond. And then I got to thinking about

131

the training nights we used to go to. Always learning one more thing. The fun of selling at the parties. I miss it all."

Jenny put the jug on and sat down. Carefully. She felt more like falling over. Where was this going?

"I think I might have been a bit rash. So I've decided, well sort of anyway, that I think I'd like to get back into party plan again," Sarah announced.

"Really?" Jenny felt a surge of excitement at the picture of how things were at the start, followed very quickly by caution. She knew better now than to react. She got back up to pour the coffees and thought for a bit. "Why do you want to come back? You didn't seem to enjoy any of the activities it took to build the business."

"What can I say? Hawaii still looks good. And I loved how you two were sharing a business interest together. I felt part of a great group at training. We were so supported, we had so much fun. Quite frankly, my life has been a bit empty and lonely since then."

Jenny's heart sunk and she took a deep breath. "Wrong reasons, Sarah." She started carefully. She didn't want to upset Sarah or knock her good intentions. "I think that's why a lot of people join party plan, because of the camaraderie I guess you'd call it. You feel a part of something. You get the best support, the best advice and you are encouraged to make mistakes as you learn, 'cos that's how you get more professional. Not your average workplace environment," she added. "But you still have to do the work. You have to make it happen. And when you first join, when you are so enthusiastic, that's the time to take massive action, because your enthusiasm pushes through your lack of confidence and your dislike of making the calls. Or asking people to have a party. Once you have a few under your belt, it definitely gets easier. And then you can go on to learning new skills. But do you know what one thing you must have, Sarah?"

Sarah was frowning. She thought she'd be welcomed back with open arms. "What?"

"You've got to have a really good reason for doing what you're doing. And I think you originally got into it because I convinced you that it was a great idea and you were infected with my enthusiasm. But that was my motivation, And that's not going to help you push yourself through your comfort zones. You have to have your own motivation. And I don't think that joining the party plan club is going to do it for you. Honestly." Jenny took a deep breath. This was one of the hardest things she'd ever had to do. Sarah was offering her friendship and the chance to do party plan together again. But Jenny couldn't go through that cycle again. And if there was one thing she'd learned through party plan, that's exactly what would happen. Unless Sarah had a really good motivation for joining. She looked up to see where

Sarah was at and her heart dropped into her boots when she saw tears in Sarah's eyes.

"It's just that you seem to be so sure of where you're going now. I've never known what I wanted to do, you know, when the kids started school. I thought that was my chance to find myself." She pulled out a tissue from her bag and blew her nose.

"But you didn't like it, Sarah. You didn't want to do any of the activities you had to do to make the business work." Jenny reminded her gently.

"I know, but I don't know what else to do! I have to do something with my life, and I love the idea of being part of a great team. I just want to feel like I belong somewhere," Sarah sniffed.

Jenny walked around the table and gave Sarah a big hug. Her friend sounded so lost and forlorn. She looked into her eyes. "So what are you going to do to find your thing, then?"

"I don't know. That's the point. I don't know where to start. Party plan seemed the easy answer. But, you're right. I don't really want to do it, I just want to be a part of it."

"Okay, well then, let's formulate a plan for you to find your mojo." Jenny was pleased to see a weak smile from Sarah.

"Do you think we can do that? By going hunting for it? Even when you don't know what you are hunting for?" Sarah was listening now. A glimmer of hope made her feel stronger than she had felt for weeks. "Where do we start?"

"Well, I've just been listening to this tape." Jenny went to the kitchen drawer and pulled out a notebook and walked into the lounge to get the CD set. "This is your first journal. And here are the CDs to listen to."

Sarah picked up a set of Cheryl Richardson's, *Finding your Passion*. My God, you're serious. You mean we can turn my search for my passion into a project? How bizarre, I would never have thought of doing that."

"Right. Take notes."

Sarah pulled a pen from her bag and waited expectantly for Jenny to sit down. She felt proud watching Jenny step so naturally into the leadership role.

"Right! Number 1: If they were going to take away all the libraries and bookshops, what sections couldn't you live without? Number 2: When you were a child, what did you used to get so excited about and dream about becoming? Number 3: What activity in your life that when you do it, do you lose track of time?" Sarah was writing furiously, trying to keep up.

"Well," she started.

"No, don't answer these now. You want to really think these through and put them in your journal. Don't try and join the dots, you might think that some of the answers have no relevance. Just write them down. All the programming we've had by well-meaning teachers, caring adults and parents, manipulating friends, means we lose the ability to be passionate about what we love. We are trained to be practical, to do what we have to, to survive. And yet, we're only living half a life. A sad, unfulfilled life."

Sarah felt tears prickling again, and she knew that Jenny had touched something deep in her heart that was yearning to find its way out. Suddenly, she felt suffocated, she needed more air in her life so she could breathe again. Deeply. That air had to come from something she felt passionate about. "Would you do something for me?"

"I'd love to say, anything. But you have to do this yourself," Jenny was quietly firm.

"Would you coach me in my search?'

Jenny blinked. "I'd be proud to," caught in her throat. And they were hugging each other, stumbling over words, laughing at themselves, in a space of honesty and courage where genuine friendship lived.

"You know," Jenny was thoughtful again as she boiled the jug to replace their cold coffees. "Do you know what the secret to success is, in my opinion?"

"Do tell," Sarah was smiling but seriously wanted to learn from Jenny.

"I think it's all about self-development. Understanding yourself and why you react the way you do. Then that knowledge gives you the discipline to push yourself through your comfort zone to try things that scare the hell out of you. And as you grow and develop, that self-awareness leads you to consciously learning new skills, which take you to the next level again. And the motivation has to come from within. You can't do it for anyone else, although," she added, "many women start out by doing party plan for their family. They think about earning extra money so they can do things for their kids. But sooner or later, they have to face the fact that ultimately, they have to do this for themselves. And that's quite confronting for us, as women. Like you, most don't know where to start."

"It's so confusing. All you know is that something is missing. And you are searching for something. I thought that I had found it in the party plan team."

"Well, we're all so supportive because we are all doing the work. We're doing the stuff behind the scenes just like you do when preparing for the dinner party. That's what we all have in common. That's the glue, which holds us all together. That's why we celebrate so heartily. That's why we recognise the bravery of someone starting out. We know the journey they're embarking on, as we've all been there. That's why international conference is so sweet. Did you know that Mark and I leave next week for Hawaii?"

Sarah smiled. "Jenny, I'm so proud of you. You've become a real professional, a real businesswomen and a fantastic role model. And I know it hasn't always been easy for you. I recognise that now. You just make it look easy. You have more courage than anyone I know. "

"Don't, you'll make me cry. You know, I'm just running my own show. And I'm really looking forward to the day when you say the same thing."

When Mark arrived home, the two of them were still sitting and full-on chatting at the table. Bursts of laughter greeted him as he walked through the door. He stopped in his tracks when he saw it was Sarah at the table. He had been expecting one of Jenny's recruits. But he hadn't heard this much warmth in Jenny's voice for a while. Sarah got up and gave him a hug. "I hear you're off to Hawaii next week. Congratulations. To both of you."

"What's going on?" He looked from one to the other. Jenny explained and finished with, "And so I'm going to coach Sarah in her journey."

Mark looked at Sarah and grinned. "Good girl. I knew you had it in you but you weren't willing to look. I think this calls for a champagne!"

As the three of them raised their glasses, the two friends looked at each other.

"Here's to running my own show!" they said in unison.

16

Coaching The Coach

When you first start building your team, remember they are not you. They have different ways of looking at things, different life experiences, and most of all, a different level of confidence. If people are lacking in self-confidence, they will be frightened of making mistakes. Telling them how you did it, will not make an impact. It will not encourage them to try it for themselves, and it won't make any sense to them if it doesn't work for them. What you have to start doing is to ask questions. Usually, if you have tried something and succeeded, you tell someone how to do what you did. If they don't do it well or it doesn't seem to work for them, what those with healthy self-esteem do is to simply tell them again what to do. But until you know why it didn't work for them, you don't know how to advise them. You can't solve the problem if you don't know what it is. When you hear the dreaded words, "It's all right for you!", you know that you are giving them your point of view, you are not seeing things from their point of view. This is when you start asking and stop telling.

**When you hear the dreaded words, "It's all right for you!",
you know that you are giving them your point of view,
you are not seeing things from their point of view.
This is when you start asking and stop telling.**

Low Self-Esteem

Low self-esteem is different from lacking in confidence, although the two very often go together. Lacking confidence just means that I don't know how to do this yet and need some support in getting through this. The bottom line is that once they have done it a couple of times, it will get easier and one success will lift that self-confidence immediately. They'll be ready to take on any number of calls. Low self-esteem is a different thing entirely. It means that you don't believe that you deserve success. Instead of separating your behaviour from your being, your value as a human being, you combine your value as a human being with your behaviour. In other words, a confident person will say, I made a mistake, I won't do that again, and their dignity as a human being remains intact. However, when a person with low self-esteem makes a mistake, they believe that it confirms that they are stupid, dumb and not worth bothering with. They'll be reluctant to start something for fear of making mistakes. And they will take all rejection personally.

What are the symptoms of low self-esteem? People with low self-esteem do not feel comfortable in the limelight so will usually not wear jewellery, make-up or make much of an effort in their presentation. They may not carry a handbag, rather always use the same old backpack or a bag they have used for years. They will not want to talk about themselves, and if you pay them a compliment, they will become very uncomfortable and think that you are only saying that because you have to. Another sign of low self-esteem, which I have noticed through my coaching, is that often people with low self-esteem can have a lot of sugar in their drinks or drink a lot of soft drinks. They don't eat or drink well and they don't look after themselves physically. In their eyes, they're not worth spending the time and effort on.

Handling Rejection

A word on handling rejection. Most of us find going up to strangers at a party and asking them to have a show, a huge challenge. This is the biggest barrier we face when we join party plan. Because we are doing something new, we lack confidence and then someone says no, and it's devastating. The shock of hearing no from family or friends whom we simply assumed would help us, is breathtaking. Wouldn't it be great if we could get our confidence up first before we have to ask someone to have a party? But it's a catch-22 situation. It's the actual asking and getting used to the answer which is the very thing which builds our confidence. So, let's explore rejection for a moment.

The shock of hearing no from family or friends whom we simply assumed would help us, is breathtaking.

Firstly, because we feel unsure and insecure, we start by assuming the next thing they are going to say, is going to be a no. So, if they say, my baby's sick, I couldn't have a party at the moment, we take that as a no. It's not. It's a "not now". And they haven't said no to you, they have said "not

138

now" to the opportunity of having a party while the baby's sick. These are two completely different things. It just feels bad. But remember, at the risk of really repeating myself, how you feel is not how you're doing!

Secondly, learning to handle rejection is what makes people successful. The most successful people in the world are the most rejected. And the least rejected, are the least successful in the world. Think about a politician who gets into government with 40 percent of votes. That may be the majority because the other parties make up the rest, but the reality is that 60 percent of people voted against him or her. That's millions and millions of people voting against them. Now, that's rejection!

No one likes to feel rejected so you need to have some strategies to get you through and make sure that it doesn't stop you in your tracks. Nothing will kill your business faster than stopping when you get a no. What you want to do is to set a goal that you won't stop until you get a yes. So you just keep calling. And this is where stats are so important. If you pull the numbers and monitor how many calls you made, or how many people you asked at the party, you will start to see a pattern. You need to do this every week so you know what your stats are.

This does three things. It keeps your focus on asking, it tells you what your stats are and it keeps you real. And it may be quite surprising. You may find that when you phone after a party, your stats are two people out of eight will book their own party. And at a party, you might find that one in five will book a party. So, once you know this, do you know what this means? That means when you call after a party, you just need to make a total of eight calls to get two parties. So when someone says no, you are one step closer to the yes. So with this knowledge, it is easier to keep going. Your energy will lift and it won't be so soul-destroying when you get another no. When you are at a party, listening very closely to what they are saying, you'll find your stats improve if you use their Emotional Connection to tempt them to have a party. If they say no, for whatever reason, that's one step closer to the person who says yes.

The sooner you can learn to move on after a no, the more quickly you will grow your business. If you wallow in how it feels to be rejected, how stupid you feel, how awkward the whole situation is, you'll wind down your energy and enthusiasm and avoid asking anyone else. And your pipeline will empty and suddenly, you'll look at the month ahead and there won't be any bookings. Because you've stopped asking.

And by the way, what do you say when they say no? If you have used the bag they think is to die for, as the hostess half-price gift, you have to ask yourself if this makes sense. Think about it. If you love a product and want it more than anything in the world, why would you turn down the opportunity to get it at half price? So when they say, no, I don't want to have a party, your next questions should be, a nice soft: "Do you mind if I ask you why you wouldn't be interested in having a party when it's going to get you your bag at half price?" You may find, that they have a mistaken idea about what they have to do to host a party. They may not want to have to do the supper.

If I were in your shoes, I'd jump right in and tell her that you'll bring the supper. Think about the sales you'll get. This will eat into your profits but less of $X is better than all of nothing. Once you remove her perceived barrier, you may just find that she agrees to host a party. What you do next is to get her to examine closely the bag she adores. Get her to sling it over her shoulder. Get her to try her wallet to make sure it fits snugly in this gorgeous bag. Really strengthen her Emotional Connection until she can't wait to get her hands on it. And make sure that you keep right on top of your hostess coaching to make sure that she doesn't get doubts and have second thoughts.

Those who learn to focus on their goals and keep trying despite some rejection, are the people most likely to move forward to success.

Doing Me The Favour

When we first start, because we are lacking in confidence, we are looking at everything from our own point of view. We are looking at everything from the "selling" point of view. But, there's a "buying" point of view also. The customer is going through a process of their own, and they will be sending out signals for us to read. However, when we are so absorbed in our own insecurities, it doesn't occur to us we might be doing the other person a disservice by not asking them to have a party, or to join the business. Here's what one successful lady told me.

"I think I would have liked to have known how easy recruiting was, and not to have been afraid of it. I joined in February and it took me until August before I finally did a "my story" bid at one of my parties — and it was at that party that I signed up my first girl. My biggest challenge was in thinking that people wouldn't want to join, so I never offered! Just think of how many lost opportunities I had in that first six months.

"Once I got my head around that I was really doing them the favour, and not them doing me a favour by joining. My business turned around tenfold, I also now always think, what will they get out of joining, not what will I get out of their joining."

Some wise words from a smart lady.

The End of the Journey

So we leave Jenny and Sarah, and your journey with them. So let's review our journey with them for a while. How have you read this book? Have you sat and read it straight through? That might work for a first reading, but this book is intended to be more than just an interesting story. Hopefully, there are skills and techniques in here that you have added to your tool kit of skills. And, I am also hoping that you will have applied something from every chapter. So, if you haven't used this book as a workbook, I'm going to suggest that you start it again and read it chapter by chapter, not moving on until you have applied the lessons from each chapter.

We have left some blank pages for you to make notes on. I would recommend that you note down what you have learned, and identify what action you are going to take to implement this new skill. And you might like to go back and write down the result of using this new skill. Because, one day you will want to train others. And if your note-taking has been this thorough, you can go back through your notes in this book to get ideas and stories you can use for your training sessions with your team.

Every chapter should have at least one action for you to apply at the end. Something you commit yourself to doing, not just something you think is interesting. If you focus on a new skill every week, in a couple of months you will be so much more skilled, but more importantly, much more confident in yourself.

Self-Honesty

The next thing to do while, during and after reading the book, is to pull up your stats and look at your results. Are you happy with your progress? Do you know how much better you're getting? Are you measuring your progress? The most simple way to do this is to get some graph paper and simply graph your results. Anything you focus on and graph, usually goes up. Simply because you are now focused on it and very aware of what you are doing.

Since you started reading the book, have you started a journal? This is where you put all your goals, your ideas, thoughts, suggestions and frustrations. My last journal lasted two years and it is always so interesting to go back and tick off your goals as you achieve them. With a red pen!

The thing, which is noticeable as you go through an old journal, is how small our goals are when we first start asking for what we want. And as we grow and stretch, so do our aspirations and goals. It also becomes a great source of ideas when you run out of them — which is one of the reasons you want to always have your journal close at hand, so you can take notes whenever something new occurs to you. Take your journal whenever you do a workshop, or go to listen to a motivation or inspiring speaker. If you keep this all together, it makes for great reading and inspiration when you need it. Keep all your favourite quotes and sayings there. Write down the name of books when you hear people recommend them. Also any websites which you think may be helpful.

Have you started a vision board where you can see it easily? Does it have pictures of the things you have set as goals on it? It's amazing how well a vision board works.

Now, if you haven't set your goals and written them down, and you haven't started a journal, haven't created a vision-board, ask yourself, "Why?" What has stopped you? And if you're giving these things to do with your teams, and they are not doing them, ask them: "Why haven't you done them?" Too busy doesn't cut it any more. What this means is that you didn't make this activity a high enough priority and you need to stop and take stock of how committed you really are to your business.

You didn't make this activity a high enough priority. You need to stop and take stock of how committed you really are to your business.

If you're not happy with your progress, what are you going to do about it? What specifically is the area that you feel is letting you down? And do not say, product knowledge. This is an indicator of lack of confidence. Have you had a meeting with your upline about it? She may very well know someone who is really good at that one thing, and that person, if asked, may be willing to mentor you. But you have to take the first step with your upline and ask.

Damn it, it always boils down to asking. You have to identify your goals and decide what it is you want to achieve, and goal-setting is simply asking for what you want.

You have to ask for what you want from life.

You have to approach people and ask them to have a party.

You have to approach people and ask them to join the business.

In fact, in this business, you have to get very good at asking.

I wish you all the success you would like to achieve. Read as much as you can, listen to as many CDs as you can. I suggest that you and your team create a self-development library or go to the public library and share the books around. Make your self-development your first priority as everything is rooted in that. And you'll find that you'll have a challenging and fulfilling life, with the great joy you get when you help others. Because the fact of the matter is, that when you are running your own show in party plan, you are helping others feel great about themselves, you are helping others have fun with their friends at parties, and last but not least, you are helping others change their lives by supporting them in running their own business also. And it doesn't get much better than that. By helping one other person, your contribution is so much more than you can imagine. By holding back and not asking them to join the business, you are not contributing to either your growth or theirs.

Good luck.

Recommended Reading

To be successful in party plan, your self-development must be a priority. I have included this list of recommended books for you to continue your development. They are all books which I have found to be useful in my own development. Some are recent books, others are old favourites.

If you can't afford to buy them new, I recommend the library system as the authors get a payment every time you borrow from the library system – if they have registered for the PLR (Public Lending Rights payment). If you simply must own it and are on a budget, or it is an old book and out of print, I recommend abebooks.com This is a global network of second-hand bookshops who are reliable, fast and economical.

Rich Dad's The Business School For People Who Like Helping People by Robert Kiyosaki with Sharon L. Lechter, C.P.A.

The Greatness Guide by Robin Sharma

Your First Year in Network Marketing, Overcome Your Fears, Experience Success, and Achieve Your Dream! By Mark Yarnell and Renee Reid Yarnell

How to Sell More Cookies, Condos, Cadillacs, Computers and Everything Else with Markita Andrews with Cheryl Merser.
Just a word about this book, Markita was six when she joined the Girl Scouts and, by age 14, had sold more than 30,000 boxes of Girl Scout cookies. Learning from this smart young lady is very sobering, especially when you realise that the lessons she has learnt in selling, are the very ones we all need to learn and adapt for ourselves whatever we are selling. If she can do it...

The One Minute Millionaire, The Enlightened Way to Wealth by Mark Victor Hanson and Robert G. Allen. I would recommend any and all books written by these two including ***The Power of Focus, How To Hit Your***

Business, Person and Financial Targets they wrote with Les Hewitt

Focal Point, A Proven System to Simplify Your Life, Double Your Productivity and Achieve Your Goals by Brian Tracy. Plus anything by Brian Tracy.

How To Get From Where You Are To Where You Want To Be by Jack Canfield. Especially principle 35 on commitment.

Plus the three great classics of all time. A must if you are serious about your self-development and/or the development of your team. Most successful people I know, have coached or have interviewed have read these books many times over. Surely that speaks for itself.

Think & Grow Rich by Napoleon Hill
The Richest Man in Babylon by George S. Clason
Man's Search for Meaning by Viktor E. Frankl

Inspiring authors
Read any of their books, just get your hands on one.

Suze Orman on money and wealth

Cheryl Richardson for finding the passion in your life and finding ways to create a happier, more balanced life.

Og Mandino for old-fashioned compassion, inspiration and taking us back to the basics of leading an ethical life.

COACH yourself to WEALTH

*Remove the invisible barriers.
Make the quantum leap!*

Shirley McKinnon

- **Have you ever wondered why some people can sell highly priced items and why others need to discount to sell?**

- **Why do so many people have such trouble in gaining control of their spending?**

- **The real reason behind credit card debt.**

Learn the answers to all these and more. Our attitude to money is usually emotionally based and forms an invisible barrier, affecting how we approach wealth creation or any decision connected with money.

This invisible barrier is why so many people have difficulty closing the sale and negotiating.

And most people don't realise they have these invisible barriers!

Order now from
www.shirleymckinnon.com

THE MONEY & MEANING CD SERIES
Professional Development for People in Business

PART ONE — **CREATING A LASER FOCUS**
Today's business environment is so full of uncertainty and
confusion, new theories, latest research and trends. Now, more than
ever, you need your own compass. Having a strong focus makes
for less-stressed business owners and more profitable businesses.
Goals add meaning to your life, raise your energy levels and get you
to where you want to go, faster. Learn why so many people do not
achieve their goals and what to do about it.

PART TWO — **MAKE MORE SALES**
Learn why so many business owners and sales people are
missing out on thousands of dollars of missed sales. Move
yourself out of survival mode and upsell every customer every time.
Why creating a desire is vital for today's customer and how to do it.
Learn the secret to becoming powerfully persuasive. Then teach these
techniques to your staff or your team.

Order now from
www.shirleymckinnon.com

HERDING CATS

for the Manager who wants to build
SALES
CHAMPIONS

HERDING CATS
A WORKBOOK FOR MANAGERS OF TEAMS
WHO DON'T HAVE TO DO A DAMN THING YOU SAY!
SHIRLEY McKINNON

Sometimes the reason the team doesn't do things that you want is because of you!

Herding Cats is a self-paced journey of self-discovery crammed full of tips and techniques from 25 years of sales and management experience by Shirley McKinnon, Australia's leading Sales and Management trainer and Master Coach.

Some quotes from the workbook:
- You are the key as to whether they stay and succeed, or simply slip away
- Be very aware of the impact your weaknesses and blind spots have on your team
- Many set goals which will move them away from what we don't want. Those who succeed set conscious goals, which they move towards.

Learn
- How to increase your Emotional Intelligence so you can manage them better, especially under stress. Usually under stress we tell more, listen less and push harder
- How to listen so they feel listened to and therefore become more motivated
- How to handle and manage your most problem people
- The subtle messages that you send your under-performers

Order now from
www.shirleymckinnon.com

Shirley McKinnon

International Author,
Speaker, Master Coach,
Leadership Trainer & Team Builder

While Shirley McKinnon is one of Australia's leading business trainers, she has many years' experience of working with party plan companies. She knows the unique challenges faced by those who join party plan, and the tremendous rewards waiting for those who are willing to push through their comfort zones and learn new skills.

As a Master Coach, Shirley's coaching has been life-changing for so many in the party plan and direct selling industries. She creates immediate and noticeable changes in the way people think and behave. Hidden barriers are revealed much to the amazement of the person being coached, although they were only too aware of the results of their barriers.

As a trainer, she has a wealth of real-life examples, which entertain, inspire and teach. Her training is a mixture of sales techniques, self-development and leadership. Her techniques are fun, practical, totally about party plan and direct selling, and they work! Shirley has an uncanny ability to infiltrate the way people think, so while the discoveries are personal, they contain valuable insights for leaders of teams. Her passion, energy and humour inject new life into the business of party plan.

An International business author, Shirley is a prolific writer on leadership and self-development and has now filled the gap so desperately needed in party plan. She explains behaviour and enables you to better understand both self and those around you.

Shirley has several books and CDs written for the party plan and direct-selling industry.

Coach Yourself to Wealth was Dymock's Business Book of the Month when published and reveals Shirley's research on why people are poor at selling and handling money. The practical exercises at the end of each chapter reveal emotional baggage around money is what Shirley calls the hidden barriers to success and wealth.

Herding Cats is a workbook for leaders of party plan or direct selling teams and network marketers. This unique and practical self-coaching manual reveals the impact of your leadership style which you may not have realised before. Understand completely the reasons behind why you impact some people positively, and others negatively.

CDs – *The Money and Meaning Series* – for people who don't have time to watch DVDs.
Creating a Laser Focus. Having a strong focus is what keeps you going when you hit resistance. What you need when you hit that soul-destroying, no. When you take your eyes off your goals, all you see are the problems. Find out why focus and goals are the foundation of your motivation and vital for your energy and well-being.

Make More Sales. Learn why so many direct-sellers are missing out on thousands of dollars of missed sales. And what to do about it. Why creating desire is vital for today's customer and how to do it. Learn the secret on how to become powerfully persuasive.

All products are available on her website www.shirleymckinnon.com
Or partyplantraining.com

To book Shirley as a dynamic speaker at your next conference, call:

08 9202 3854

or email shirley@shirleymckinnon.com

www.ingramcontent.com/pod-product-compliance
Lightning Source LLC
Chambersburg PA
CBHW051525170526
45165CB00002B/609